THIS IS YOUR **PASSBOOK**® FOR ...

RECREATION SPECIALIST

NATIONAL LEARNING CORPORATION®
passbooks.com

Copyright © 2020 by

NLC®

National Learning Corporation

212 Michael Drive, Syosset, NY 11791
(516) 921-8888 • www.passbooks.com
E-mail: info@passbooks.com

PUBLISHED IN THE UNITED STATES OF AMERICA

PASSBOOK® SERIES

THE *PASSBOOK® SERIES* has been created to prepare applicants and candidates for the ultimate academic battlefield – the examination room.

At some time in our lives, each and every one of us may be required to take an examination – for validation, matriculation, admission, qualification, registration, certification, or licensure.

Based on the assumption that every applicant or candidate has met the basic formal educational standards, has taken the required number of courses, and read the necessary texts, the *PASSBOOK® SERIES* furnishes the one special preparation which may assure passing with confidence, instead of failing with insecurity. Examination questions – together with answers – are furnished as the basic vehicle for study so that the mysteries of the examination and its compounding difficulties may be eliminated or diminished by a sure method.

This book is meant to help you pass your examination provided that you qualify and are serious in your objective.

The entire field is reviewed through the huge store of content information which is succinctly presented through a provocative and challenging approach – the question-and-answer method.

A climate of success is established by furnishing the correct answers at the end of each test.

You soon learn to recognize types of questions, forms of questions, and patterns of questioning. You may even begin to anticipate expected outcomes.

You perceive that many questions are repeated or adapted so that you can gain acute insights, which may enable you to score many sure points.

You learn how to confront new questions, or types of questions, and to attack them confidently and work out the correct answers.

You note objectives and emphases, and recognize pitfalls and dangers, so that you may make positive educational adjustments.

Moreover, you are kept fully informed in relation to new concepts, methods, practices, and directions in the field.

You discover that you arre actually taking the examination all the time: you are preparing for the examination by "taking" an examination, not by reading extraneous and/or supererogatory textbooks.

In short, this PASSBOOK®, used directedly, should be an important factor in helping you to pass your test.

RECREATION SPECIALIST

DUTIES:
Leads or instructs in specialized fields of recreation; performs related duties as required.

SUBJECT OF EXAMINATION:
The written test designed to evaluate knowledge, skills and /or abilities in the following areas:

1. **Office record keeping** - These questions test your ability to perform common office record keeping tasks. The test consists of two or more "sets" of questions, each set concerning a different problem. Typical record keeping problems might involve the organization or collation of data from several sources; scheduling; maintaining a record system using running balances; or completion of a table summarizing data using totals, subtotals, averages and percents.

2. **Principles and practices of leisure recreation** - These questions test for a knowledge of the basic concepts and common practices employed in the planning and implementation of leisure-time recreation programs in athletics, social activities, and avocational interests. Questions may cover such areas as program/activity planning for the major user groups, program/activity planning for people with special needs; operation of recreation areas, recreation center buildings, and specialized recreation facilities (pools, tennis courts, etc.); and scheduling of activities.

3. **Working with people to facilitate recreation and/or leisure activities** - These questions will test for the knowledge and abilities necessary to work with individuals of all backgrounds in the context of providing recreation and leisure activities. Questions may cover such areas as: human behavior and development, handling difficult situations, engaging and motivating participants, building rapport with participants, working with volunteers, and planning appropriate activities for participant group.

HOW TO TAKE A TEST

I. YOU MUST PASS AN EXAMINATION

A. WHAT EVERY CANDIDATE SHOULD KNOW

Examination applicants often ask us for help in preparing for the written test. What can I study in advance? What kinds of questions will be asked? How will the test be given? How will the papers be graded?

As an applicant for a civil service examination, you may be wondering about some of these things. Our purpose here is to suggest effective methods of advance study and to describe civil service examinations.

Your chances for success on this examination can be increased if you know how to prepare. Those "pre-examination jitters" can be reduced if you know what to expect. You can even experience an adventure in good citizenship if you know why civil service exams are given.

B. WHY ARE CIVIL SERVICE EXAMINATIONS GIVEN?

Civil service examinations are important to you in two ways. As a citizen, you want public jobs filled by employees who know how to do their work. As a job seeker, you want a fair chance to compete for that job on an equal footing with other candidates. The best-known means of accomplishing this two-fold goal is the competitive examination.

Exams are widely publicized throughout the nation. They may be administered for jobs in federal, state, city, municipal, town or village governments or agencies.

Any citizen may apply, with some limitations, such as the age or residence of applicants. Your experience and education may be reviewed to see whether you meet the requirements for the particular examination. When these requirements exist, they are reasonable and applied consistently to all applicants. Thus, a competitive examination may cause you some uneasiness now, but it is your privilege and safeguard.

C. HOW ARE CIVIL SERVICE EXAMS DEVELOPED?

Examinations are carefully written by trained technicians who are specialists in the field known as "psychological measurement," in consultation with recognized authorities in the field of work that the test will cover. These experts recommend the subject matter areas or skills to be tested; only those knowledges or skills important to your success on the job are included. The most reliable books and source materials available are used as references. Together, the experts and technicians judge the difficulty level of the questions.

Test technicians know how to phrase questions so that the problem is clearly stated. Their ethics do not permit "trick" or "catch" questions. Questions may have been tried out on sample groups, or subjected to statistical analysis, to determine their usefulness.

Written tests are often used in combination with performance tests, ratings of training and experience, and oral interviews. All of these measures combine to form the best-known means of finding the right person for the right job.

II. HOW TO PASS THE WRITTEN TEST

A. NATURE OF THE EXAMINATION

To prepare intelligently for civil service examinations, you should know how they differ from school examinations you have taken. In school you were assigned certain definite pages to read or subjects to cover. The examination questions were quite detailed and usually emphasized memory. Civil service exams, on the other hand, try to discover your present ability to perform the duties of a position, plus your potentiality to learn these duties. In other words, a civil service exam attempts to predict how successful you will be. Questions cover such a broad area that they cannot be as minute and detailed as school exam questions.

In the public service similar kinds of work, or positions, are grouped together in one "class." This process is known as *position-classification*. All the positions in a class are paid according to the salary range for that class. One class title covers all of these positions, and they are all tested by the same examination.

B. FOUR BASIC STEPS

1) Study the announcement

How, then, can you know what subjects to study? Our best answer is: "Learn as much as possible about the class of positions for which you've applied." The exam will test the knowledge, skills and abilities needed to do the work.

Your most valuable source of information about the position you want is the official exam announcement. This announcement lists the training and experience qualifications. Check these standards and apply only if you come reasonably close to meeting them.

The brief description of the position in the examination announcement offers some clues to the subjects which will be tested. Think about the job itself. Review the duties in your mind. Can you perform them, or are there some in which you are rusty? Fill in the blank spots in your preparation.

Many jurisdictions preview the written test in the exam announcement by including a section called "Knowledge and Abilities Required," "Scope of the Examination," or some similar heading. Here you will find out specifically what fields will be tested.

2) Review your own background

Once you learn in general what the position is all about, and what you need to know to do the work, ask yourself which subjects you already know fairly well and which need improvement. You may wonder whether to concentrate on improving your strong areas or on building some background in your fields of weakness. When the announcement has specified "some knowledge" or "considerable knowledge," or has used adjectives like "beginning principles of..." or "advanced ... methods," you can get a clue as to the number and difficulty of questions to be asked in any given field. More questions, and hence broader coverage, would be included for those subjects which are more important in the work. Now weigh your strengths and weaknesses against the job requirements and prepare accordingly.

3) Determine the level of the position

Another way to tell how intensively you should prepare is to understand the level of the job for which you are applying. Is it the entering level? In other words, is this the position in which beginners in a field of work are hired? Or is it an intermediate or advanced level? Sometimes this is indicated by such words as "Junior" or "Senior" in the class title. Other jurisdictions use Roman numerals to designate the level – Clerk I, Clerk II, for example. The word "Supervisor" sometimes appears in the title. If the level is not indicated by the title, check the description of duties. Will you be working under very close supervision, or will you have responsibility for independent decisions in this work?

4) Choose appropriate study materials

Now that you know the subjects to be examined and the relative amount of each subject to be covered, you can choose suitable study materials. For beginning level jobs, or even advanced ones, if you have a pronounced weakness in some aspect of your training, read a modern, standard textbook in that field. Be sure it is up to date and has general coverage. Such books are normally available at your library, and the librarian will be glad to help you locate one. For entry-level positions, questions of appropriate difficulty are chosen – neither highly advanced questions, nor those too simple. Such questions require careful thought but not advanced training.

If the position for which you are applying is technical or advanced, you will read more advanced, specialized material. If you are already familiar with the basic principles of your field, elementary textbooks would waste your time. Concentrate on advanced textbooks and technical periodicals. Think through the concepts and review difficult problems in your field.

These are all general sources. You can get more ideas on your own initiative, following these leads. For example, training manuals and publications of the government agency which employs workers in your field can be useful, particularly for technical and professional positions. A letter or visit to the government department involved may result in more specific study suggestions, and certainly will provide you with a more definite idea of the exact nature of the position you are seeking.

III. KINDS OF TESTS

Tests are used for purposes other than measuring knowledge and ability to perform specified duties. For some positions, it is equally important to test ability to make adjustments to new situations or to profit from training. In others, basic mental abilities not dependent on information are essential. Questions which test these things may not appear as pertinent to the duties of the position as those which test for knowledge and information. Yet they are often highly important parts of a fair examination. For very general questions, it is almost impossible to help you direct your study efforts. What we can do is to point out some of the more common of these general abilities needed in public service positions and describe some typical questions.

1) General information

Broad, general information has been found useful for predicting job success in some kinds of work. This is tested in a variety of ways, from vocabulary lists to questions about current events. Basic background in some field of work, such as sociology or economics, may be sampled in a group of questions. Often these are principles which have become familiar to most persons through exposure rather than through formal training. It is difficult to advise you how to study for these questions; being alert to the world around you is our best suggestion.

2) Verbal ability

An example of an ability needed in many positions is verbal or language ability. Verbal ability is, in brief, the ability to use and understand words. Vocabulary and grammar tests are typical measures of this ability. Reading comprehension or paragraph interpretation questions are common in many kinds of civil service tests. You are given a paragraph of written material and asked to find its central meaning.

3) Numerical ability

Number skills can be tested by the familiar arithmetic problem, by checking paired lists of numbers to see which are alike and which are different, or by interpreting charts and graphs. In the latter test, a graph may be printed in the test booklet which you are asked to use as the basis for answering questions.

4) Observation

A popular test for law-enforcement positions is the observation test. A picture is shown to you for several minutes, then taken away. Questions about the picture test your ability to observe both details and larger elements.

5) Following directions

In many positions in the public service, the employee must be able to carry out written instructions dependably and accurately. You may be given a chart with several columns, each column listing a variety of information. The questions require you to carry out directions involving the information given in the chart.

6) Skills and aptitudes

Performance tests effectively measure some manual skills and aptitudes. When the skill is one in which you are trained, such as typing or shorthand, you can practice. These tests are often very much like those given in business school or high school courses. For many of the other skills and aptitudes, however, no short-time preparation can be made. Skills and abilities natural to you or that you have developed throughout your lifetime are being tested.

Many of the general questions just described provide all the data needed to answer the questions and ask you to use your reasoning ability to find the answers. Your best preparation for these tests, as well as for tests of facts and ideas, is to be at your physical and mental best. You, no doubt, have your own methods of getting into an exam-taking mood and keeping "in shape." The next section lists some ideas on this subject.

IV. KINDS OF QUESTIONS

Only rarely is the "essay" question, which you answer in narrative form, used in civil service tests. Civil service tests are usually of the short-answer type. Full instructions for answering these questions will be given to you at the examination. But in case this is your first experience with short-answer questions and separate answer sheets, here is what you need to know:

1) Multiple-choice Questions

Most popular of the short-answer questions is the "multiple choice" or "best answer" question. It can be used, for example, to test for factual knowledge, ability to solve problems or judgment in meeting situations found at work.

A multiple-choice question is normally one of three types—

- It can begin with an incomplete statement followed by several possible endings. You are to find the one ending which *best* completes the statement, although some of the others may not be entirely wrong.
- It can also be a complete statement in the form of a question which is answered by choosing one of the statements listed.
- It can be in the form of a problem – again you select the best answer.

Here is an example of a multiple-choice question with a discussion which should give you some clues as to the method for choosing the right answer:

When an employee has a complaint about his assignment, the action which will *best* help him overcome his difficulty is to
- A. discuss his difficulty with his coworkers
- B. take the problem to the head of the organization
- C. take the problem to the person who gave him the assignment
- D. say nothing to anyone about his complaint

In answering this question, you should study each of the choices to find which is best. Consider choice "A" – Certainly an employee may discuss his complaint with fellow employees, but no change or improvement can result, and the complaint remains unresolved. Choice "B" is a poor choice since the head of the organization probably does not know what assignment you have been given, and taking your problem to him is known as "going over the head" of the supervisor. The supervisor, or person who made the assignment, is the person who can clarify it or correct any injustice. Choice "C" is, therefore, correct. To say nothing, as in choice "D," is unwise. Supervisors have and interest in knowing the problems employees are facing, and the employee is seeking a solution to his problem.

2) True/False Questions

The "true/false" or "right/wrong" form of question is sometimes used. Here a complete statement is given. Your job is to decide whether the statement is right or wrong.

SAMPLE: A roaming cell-phone call to a nearby city costs less than a non-roaming call to a distant city.

This statement is wrong, or false, since roaming calls are more expensive.

This is not a complete list of all possible question forms, although most of the others are variations of these common types. You will always get complete directions for answering questions. Be sure you understand *how* to mark your answers – ask questions until you do.

V. RECORDING YOUR ANSWERS

Computer terminals are used more and more today for many different kinds of exams.

For an examination with very few applicants, you may be told to record your answers in the test booklet itself. Separate answer sheets are much more common. If this separate answer sheet is to be scored by machine – and this is often the case – it is highly important that you mark your answers correctly in order to get credit.

An electronic scoring machine is often used in civil service offices because of the speed with which papers can be scored. Machine-scored answer sheets must be marked with a pencil, which will be given to you. This pencil has a high graphite content which responds to the electronic scoring machine. As a matter of fact, stray dots may register as answers, so do not let your pencil rest on the answer sheet while you are pondering the correct answer. Also, if your pencil lead breaks or is otherwise defective, ask for another.

Since the answer sheet will be dropped in a slot in the scoring machine, be careful not to bend the corners or get the paper crumpled.

The answer sheet normally has five vertical columns of numbers, with 30 numbers to a column. These numbers correspond to the question numbers in your test booklet. After each number, going across the page are four or five pairs of dotted lines. These short dotted lines have small letters or numbers above them. The first two pairs may also have a "T" or "F" above the letters. This indicates that the first two pairs only are to be used if the questions are of the true-false type. If the questions are multiple choice, disregard the "T" and "F" and pay attention only to the small letters or numbers.

Answer your questions in the manner of the sample that follows:

32. The largest city in the United States is
    A. Washington, D.C.
    B. New York City
    C. Chicago
    D. Detroit
    E. San Francisco

1) Choose the answer you think is best. (New York City is the largest, so "B" is correct.)
2) Find the row of dotted lines numbered the same as the question you are answering. (Find row number 32)
3) Find the pair of dotted lines corresponding to the answer. (Find the pair of lines under the mark "B.")
4) Make a solid black mark between the dotted lines.

VI. BEFORE THE TEST

Common sense will help you find procedures to follow to get ready for an examination. Too many of us, however, overlook these sensible measures. Indeed, nervousness and fatigue have been found to be the most serious reasons why applicants fail to do their best on civil service tests. Here is a list of reminders:

- Begin your preparation early – Don't wait until the last minute to go scurrying around for books and materials or to find out what the position is all about.
- Prepare continuously – An hour a night for a week is better than an all-night cram session. This has been definitely established. What is more, a night a week for a month will return better dividends than crowding your study into a shorter period of time.
- Locate the place of the exam – You have been sent a notice telling you when and where to report for the examination. If the location is in a different town or otherwise unfamiliar to you, it would be well to inquire the best route and learn something about the building.
- Relax the night before the test – Allow your mind to rest. Do not study at all that night. Plan some mild recreation or diversion; then go to bed early and get a good night's sleep.
- Get up early enough to make a leisurely trip to the place for the test – This way unforeseen events, traffic snarls, unfamiliar buildings, etc. will not upset you.
- Dress comfortably – A written test is not a fashion show. You will be known by number and not by name, so wear something comfortable.
- Leave excess paraphernalia at home – Shopping bags and odd bundles will get in your way. You need bring only the items mentioned in the official notice you received; usually everything you need is provided. Do not bring reference books to the exam. They will only confuse those last minutes and be taken away from you when in the test room.
- Arrive somewhat ahead of time – If because of transportation schedules you must get there very early, bring a newspaper or magazine to take your mind off yourself while waiting.
- Locate the examination room – When you have found the proper room, you will be directed to the seat or part of the room where you will sit. Sometimes you are given a sheet of instructions to read while you are waiting. Do not fill out any forms until you are told to do so; just read them and be prepared.
- Relax and prepare to listen to the instructions
- If you have any physical problem that may keep you from doing your best, be sure to tell the test administrator. If you are sick or in poor health, you really cannot do your best on the exam. You can come back and take the test some other time.

VII. AT THE TEST

The day of the test is here and you have the test booklet in your hand. The temptation to get going is very strong. Caution! There is more to success than knowing the right answers. You must know how to identify your papers and understand variations in the type of short-answer question used in this particular examination. Follow these suggestions for maximum results from your efforts:

1) Cooperate with the monitor

The test administrator has a duty to create a situation in which you can be as much at ease as possible. He will give instructions, tell you when to begin, check to see that you are marking your answer sheet correctly, and so on. He is not there to guard you, although he will see that your competitors do not take unfair advantage. He wants to help you do your best.

2) Listen to all instructions

Don't jump the gun! Wait until you understand all directions. In most civil service tests you get more time than you need to answer the questions. So don't be in a hurry. Read each word of instructions until you clearly understand the meaning. Study the examples, listen to all announcements and follow directions. Ask questions if you do not understand what to do.

3) Identify your papers

Civil service exams are usually identified by number only. You will be assigned a number; you must not put your name on your test papers. Be sure to copy your number correctly. Since more than one exam may be given, copy your exact examination title.

4) Plan your time

Unless you are told that a test is a "speed" or "rate of work" test, speed itself is usually not important. Time enough to answer all the questions will be provided, but this does not mean that you have all day. An overall time limit has been set. Divide the total time (in minutes) by the number of questions to determine the approximate time you have for each question.

5) Do not linger over difficult questions

If you come across a difficult question, mark it with a paper clip (useful to have along) and come back to it when you have been through the booklet. One caution if you do this – be sure to skip a number on your answer sheet as well. Check often to be sure that you have not lost your place and that you are marking in the row numbered the same as the question you are answering.

6) Read the questions

Be sure you know what the question asks! Many capable people are unsuccessful because they failed to *read* the questions correctly.

7) Answer all questions

Unless you have been instructed that a penalty will be deducted for incorrect answers, it is better to guess than to omit a question.

8) Speed tests

It is often better NOT to guess on speed tests. It has been found that on timed tests people are tempted to spend the last few seconds before time is called in marking answers at random – without even reading them – in the hope of picking up a few extra points. To discourage this practice, the instructions may warn you that your score will be "corrected" for guessing. That is, a penalty will be applied. The incorrect answers will be deducted from the correct ones, or some other penalty formula will be used.

9) Review your answers

If you finish before time is called, go back to the questions you guessed or omitted to give them further thought. Review other answers if you have time.

10) Return your test materials

If you are ready to leave before others have finished or time is called, take ALL your materials to the monitor and leave quietly. Never take any test material with you. The monitor can discover whose papers are not complete, and taking a test booklet may be grounds for disqualification.

VIII. EXAMINATION TECHNIQUES

1) Read the general instructions carefully. These are usually printed on the first page of the exam booklet. As a rule, these instructions refer to the timing of the examination; the fact that you should not start work until the signal and must stop work at a signal, etc. If there are any *special* instructions, such as a choice of questions to be answered, make sure that you note this instruction carefully.

2) When you are ready to start work on the examination, that is as soon as the signal has been given, read the instructions to each question booklet, underline any key words or phrases, such as *least*, *best*, *outline*, *describe* and the like. In this way you will tend to answer as requested rather than discover on reviewing your paper that you *listed without describing*, that you selected the *worst* choice rather than the *best* choice, etc.

3) If the examination is of the objective or multiple-choice type – that is, each question will also give a series of possible answers: A, B, C or D, and you are called upon to select the best answer and write the letter next to that answer on your answer paper – it is advisable to start answering each question in turn. There may be anywhere from 50 to 100 such questions in the three or four hours allotted and you can see how much time would be taken if you read through all the questions before beginning to answer any. Furthermore, if you come across a question or group of questions which you know would be difficult to answer, it would undoubtedly affect your handling of all the other questions.

4) If the examination is of the essay type and contains but a few questions, it is a moot point as to whether you should read all the questions before starting to answer any one. Of course, if you are given a choice – say five out of seven and the like – then it is essential to read all the questions so you can eliminate the two that are most difficult. If, however, you are asked to answer all the questions, there may be danger in trying to answer the easiest one first because you may find that you will spend too much time on it. The best technique is to answer the first question, then proceed to the second, etc.

5) Time your answers. Before the exam begins, write down the time it started, then add the time allowed for the examination and write down the time it must be completed, then divide the time available somewhat as follows:

- If 3-1/2 hours are allowed, that would be 210 minutes. If you have 80 objective-type questions, that would be an average of 2-1/2 minutes per question. Allow yourself no more than 2 minutes per question, or a total of 160 minutes, which will permit about 50 minutes to review.
- If for the time allotment of 210 minutes there are 7 essay questions to answer, that would average about 30 minutes a question. Give yourself only 25 minutes per question so that you have about 35 minutes to review.

6) The most important instruction is to *read each question* and make sure you know what is wanted. The second most important instruction is to *time yourself properly* so that you answer every question. The third most important instruction is to *answer every question*. Guess if you have to but include something for each question. Remember that you will receive no credit for a blank and will probably receive some credit if you write something in answer to an essay question. If you guess a letter – say "B" for a multiple-choice question – you may have guessed right. If you leave a blank as an answer to a multiple-choice question, the examiners may respect your feelings but it will not add a point to your score. Some exams may penalize you for wrong answers, so in such cases *only*, you may not want to guess unless you have some basis for your answer.

7) Suggestions
   a. Objective-type questions
      1. Examine the question booklet for proper sequence of pages and questions
      2. Read all instructions carefully
      3. Skip any question which seems too difficult; return to it after all other questions have been answered
      4. Apportion your time properly; do not spend too much time on any single question or group of questions
      5. Note and underline key words – *all, most, fewest, least, best, worst, same, opposite,* etc.
      6. Pay particular attention to negatives
      7. Note unusual option, e.g., unduly long, short, complex, different or similar in content to the body of the question
      8. Observe the use of "hedging" words – *probably, may, most likely,* etc.
      9. Make sure that your answer is put next to the same number as the question
      10. Do not second-guess unless you have good reason to believe the second answer is definitely more correct
      11. Cross out original answer if you decide another answer is more accurate; do not erase until you are ready to hand your paper in
      12. Answer all questions; guess unless instructed otherwise
      13. Leave time for review

   b. Essay questions
      1. Read each question carefully
      2. Determine exactly what is wanted. Underline key words or phrases.
      3. Decide on outline or paragraph answer

4. Include many different points and elements unless asked to develop any one or two points or elements
5. Show impartiality by giving pros and cons unless directed to select one side only
6. Make and write down any assumptions you find necessary to answer the questions
7. Watch your English, grammar, punctuation and choice of words
8. Time your answers; don't crowd material

8) Answering the essay question

Most essay questions can be answered by framing the specific response around several key words or ideas. Here are a few such key words or ideas:

M's: manpower, materials, methods, money, management
P's: purpose, program, policy, plan, procedure, practice, problems, pitfalls, personnel, public relations
  a. Six basic steps in handling problems:
    1. Preliminary plan and background development
    2. Collect information, data and facts
    3. Analyze and interpret information, data and facts
    4. Analyze and develop solutions as well as make recommendations
    5. Prepare report and sell recommendations
    6. Install recommendations and follow up effectiveness

  b. Pitfalls to avoid
    1. *Taking things for granted* – A statement of the situation does not necessarily imply that each of the elements is necessarily true; for example, a complaint may be invalid and biased so that all that can be taken for granted is that a complaint has been registered
    2. *Considering only one side of a situation* – Wherever possible, indicate several alternatives and then point out the reasons you selected the best one
    3. *Failing to indicate follow up* – Whenever your answer indicates action on your part, make certain that you will take proper follow-up action to see how successful your recommendations, procedures or actions turn out to be
    4. *Taking too long in answering any single question* – Remember to time your answers properly

IX. AFTER THE TEST

Scoring procedures differ in detail among civil service jurisdictions although the general principles are the same. Whether the papers are hand-scored or graded by machine we have described, they are nearly always graded by number. That is, the person who marks the paper knows only the number – never the name – of the applicant. Not until all the papers have been graded will they be matched with names. If other tests, such as training and experience or oral interview ratings have been given, scores will be combined. Different parts of the examination usually have different weights. For example, the written test might count 60 percent of the final grade, and a rating of training and experience 40 percent. In many jurisdictions, veterans will have a certain number of points added to their grades.

After the final grade has been determined, the names are placed in grade order and an eligible list is established. There are various methods for resolving ties between those who get the same final grade – probably the most common is to place first the name of the person whose application was received first. Job offers are made from the eligible list in the order the names appear on it. You will be notified of your grade and your rank as soon as all these computations have been made. This will be done as rapidly as possible.

People who are found to meet the requirements in the announcement are called "eligibles." Their names are put on a list of eligible candidates. An eligible's chances of getting a job depend on how high he stands on this list and how fast agencies are filling jobs from the list.

When a job is to be filled from a list of eligibles, the agency asks for the names of people on the list of eligibles for that job. When the civil service commission receives this request, it sends to the agency the names of the three people highest on this list. Or, if the job to be filled has specialized requirements, the office sends the agency the names of the top three persons who meet these requirements from the general list.

The appointing officer makes a choice from among the three people whose names were sent to him. If the selected person accepts the appointment, the names of the others are put back on the list to be considered for future openings.

That is the rule in hiring from all kinds of eligible lists, whether they are for typist, carpenter, chemist, or something else. For every vacancy, the appointing officer has his choice of any one of the top three eligibles on the list. This explains why the person whose name is on top of the list sometimes does not get an appointment when some of the persons lower on the list do. If the appointing officer chooses the second or third eligible, the No. 1 eligible does not get a job at once, but stays on the list until he is appointed or the list is terminated.

X. HOW TO PASS THE INTERVIEW TEST

The examination for which you applied requires an oral interview test. You have already taken the written test and you are now being called for the interview test – the final part of the formal examination.

You may think that it is not possible to prepare for an interview test and that there are no procedures to follow during an interview. Our purpose is to point out some things you can do in advance that will help you and some good rules to follow and pitfalls to avoid while you are being interviewed.

What is an interview supposed to test?

The written examination is designed to test the technical knowledge and competence of the candidate; the oral is designed to evaluate intangible qualities, not readily measured otherwise, and to establish a list showing the relative fitness of each candidate – as measured against his competitors – for the position sought. Scoring is not on the basis of "right" and "wrong," but on a sliding scale of values ranging from "not passable" to "outstanding." As a matter of fact, it is possible to achieve a relatively low score without a single "incorrect" answer because of evident weakness in the qualities being measured.

Occasionally, an examination may consist entirely of an oral test – either an individual or a group oral. In such cases, information is sought concerning the technical knowledges and abilities of the candidate, since there has been no written examination for this purpose. More commonly, however, an oral test is used to supplement a written examination.

Who conducts interviews?

The composition of oral boards varies among different jurisdictions. In nearly all, a representative of the personnel department serves as chairman. One of the members of the board may be a representative of the department in which the candidate would work. In some cases, "outside experts" are used, and, frequently, a businessman or some other representative of the general public is asked to serve. Labor and management or other special groups may be represented. The aim is to secure the services of experts in the appropriate field.

However the board is composed, it is a good idea (and not at all improper or unethical) to ascertain in advance of the interview who the members are and what groups they represent. When you are introduced to them, you will have some idea of their backgrounds and interests, and at least you will not stutter and stammer over their names.

What should be done before the interview?

While knowledge about the board members is useful and takes some of the surprise element out of the interview, there is other preparation which is more substantive. It *is* possible to prepare for an oral interview – in several ways:

1) Keep a copy of your application and review it carefully before the interview

This may be the only document before the oral board, and the starting point of the interview. Know what education and experience you have listed there, and the sequence and dates of all of it. Sometimes the board will ask you to review the highlights of your experience for them; you should not have to hem and haw doing it.

2) Study the class specification and the examination announcement

Usually, the oral board has one or both of these to guide them. The qualities, characteristics or knowledges required by the position sought are stated in these documents. They offer valuable clues as to the nature of the oral interview. For example, if the job involves supervisory responsibilities, the announcement will usually indicate that knowledge of modern supervisory methods and the qualifications of the candidate as a supervisor will be tested. If so, you can expect such questions, frequently in the form of a hypothetical situation which you are expected to solve. NEVER go into an oral without knowledge of the duties and responsibilities of the job you seek.

3) Think through each qualification required

Try to visualize the kind of questions you would ask if you were a board member. How well could you answer them? Try especially to appraise your own knowledge and background in each area, *measured against the job sought*, and identify any areas in which you are weak. Be critical and realistic – do not flatter yourself.

4) Do some general reading in areas in which you feel you may be weak

For example, if the job involves supervision and your past experience has NOT, some general reading in supervisory methods and practices, particularly in the field of human relations, might be useful. Do NOT study agency procedures or detailed manuals. The oral board will be testing your understanding and capacity, not your memory.

5) Get a good night's sleep and watch your general health and mental attitude

You will want a clear head at the interview. Take care of a cold or any other minor ailment, and of course, no hangovers.

What should be done on the day of the interview?

Now comes the day of the interview itself. Give yourself plenty of time to get there. Plan to arrive somewhat ahead of the scheduled time, particularly if your appointment is in the fore part of the day. If a previous candidate fails to appear, the board might be ready for you a bit early. By early afternoon an oral board is almost invariably behind schedule if there are many candidates, and you may have to wait. Take along a book or magazine to read, or your application to review, but leave any extraneous material in the waiting room when you go in for your interview. In any event, relax and compose yourself.

The matter of dress is important. The board is forming impressions about you – from your experience, your manners, your attitude, and your appearance. Give your personal appearance careful attention. Dress your best, but not your flashiest. Choose conservative, appropriate clothing, and be sure it is immaculate. This is a business interview, and your appearance should indicate that you regard it as such. Besides, being well groomed and properly dressed will help boost your confidence.

Sooner or later, someone will call your name and escort you into the interview room. *This is it.* From here on you are on your own. It is too late for any more preparation. But remember, you asked for this opportunity to prove your fitness, and you are here because your request was granted.

What happens when you go in?

The usual sequence of events will be as follows: The clerk (who is often the board stenographer) will introduce you to the chairman of the oral board, who will introduce you to the other members of the board. Acknowledge the introductions before you sit down. Do not be surprised if you find a microphone facing you or a stenotypist sitting by. Oral interviews are usually recorded in the event of an appeal or other review.

Usually the chairman of the board will open the interview by reviewing the highlights of your education and work experience from your application – primarily for the benefit of the other members of the board, as well as to get the material into the record. Do not interrupt or comment unless there is an error or significant misinterpretation; if that is the case, do not hesitate. But do not quibble about insignificant matters. Also, he will usually ask you some question about your education, experience or your present job – partly to get you to start talking and to establish the interviewing "rapport." He may start the actual questioning, or turn it over to one of the other members. Frequently, each member undertakes the questioning on a particular area, one in which he is perhaps most competent, so you can expect each member to participate in the examination. Because time is limited, you may also expect some rather abrupt switches in the direction the questioning takes, so do not be upset by it. Normally, a board member will not pursue a single line of questioning unless he discovers a particular strength or weakness.

After each member has participated, the chairman will usually ask whether any member has any further questions, then will ask you if you have anything you wish to add. Unless you are expecting this question, it may floor you. Worse, it may start you off on an extended, extemporaneous speech. The board is not usually seeking more information. The question is principally to offer you a last opportunity to present further qualifications or to indicate that you have nothing to add. So, if you feel that a significant qualification or characteristic has been overlooked, it is proper to point it out in a sentence or so. Do not compliment the board on the thoroughness of their examination – they have been sketchy, and you know it. If you wish, merely say, "No thank you, I have nothing further to add." This is a point where you can "talk yourself out" of a good impression or fail to present an important bit of information. Remember, *you close the interview yourself.*

The chairman will then say, "That is all, Mr. _____, thank you." Do not be startled; the interview is over, and quicker than you think. Thank him, gather your belongings and take your leave. Save your sigh of relief for the other side of the door.

How to put your best foot forward

Throughout this entire process, you may feel that the board individually and collectively is trying to pierce your defenses, seek out your hidden weaknesses and embarrass and confuse you. Actually, this is not true. They are obliged to make an appraisal of your qualifications for the job you are seeking, and they want to see you in your best light. Remember, they must interview all candidates and a non-cooperative candidate may become a failure in spite of their best efforts to bring out his qualifications. Here are 15 suggestions that will help you:

1) Be natural – Keep your attitude confident, not cocky

If you are not confident that you can do the job, do not expect the board to be. Do not apologize for your weaknesses, try to bring out your strong points. The board is interested in a positive, not negative, presentation. Cockiness will antagonize any board member and make him wonder if you are covering up a weakness by a false show of strength.

2) Get comfortable, but don't lounge or sprawl

Sit erectly but not stiffly. A careless posture may lead the board to conclude that you are careless in other things, or at least that you are not impressed by the importance of the occasion. Either conclusion is natural, even if incorrect. Do not fuss with your clothing, a pencil or an ashtray. Your hands may occasionally be useful to emphasize a point; do not let them become a point of distraction.

3) Do not wisecrack or make small talk

This is a serious situation, and your attitude should show that you consider it as such. Further, the time of the board is limited – they do not want to waste it, and neither should you.

4) Do not exaggerate your experience or abilities

In the first place, from information in the application or other interviews and sources, the board may know more about you than you think. Secondly, you probably will not get away with it. An experienced board is rather adept at spotting such a situation, so do not take the chance.

5) If you know a board member, do not make a point of it, yet do not hide it

Certainly you are not fooling him, and probably not the other members of the board. Do not try to take advantage of your acquaintanceship – it will probably do you little good.

6) Do not dominate the interview

Let the board do that. They will give you the clues – do not assume that you have to do all the talking. Realize that the board has a number of questions to ask you, and do not try to take up all the interview time by showing off your extensive knowledge of the answer to the first one.

7) Be attentive

You only have 20 minutes or so, and you should keep your attention at its sharpest throughout. When a member is addressing a problem or question to you, give him your undivided attention. Address your reply principally to him, but do not exclude the other board members.

8) Do not interrupt

A board member may be stating a problem for you to analyze. He will ask you a question when the time comes. Let him state the problem, and wait for the question.

9) Make sure you understand the question

Do not try to answer until you are sure what the question is. If it is not clear, restate it in your own words or ask the board member to clarify it for you. However, do not haggle about minor elements.

10) Reply promptly but not hastily

A common entry on oral board rating sheets is "candidate responded readily," or "candidate hesitated in replies." Respond as promptly and quickly as you can, but do not jump to a hasty, ill-considered answer.

11) Do not be peremptory in your answers

A brief answer is proper – but do not fire your answer back. That is a losing game from your point of view. The board member can probably ask questions much faster than you can answer them.

12) Do not try to create the answer you think the board member wants

He is interested in what kind of mind you have and how it works – not in playing games. Furthermore, he can usually spot this practice and will actually grade you down on it.

13) Do not switch sides in your reply merely to agree with a board member

Frequently, a member will take a contrary position merely to draw you out and to see if you are willing and able to defend your point of view. Do not start a debate, yet do not surrender a good position. If a position is worth taking, it is worth defending.

14) Do not be afraid to admit an error in judgment if you are shown to be wrong

The board knows that you are forced to reply without any opportunity for careful consideration. Your answer may be demonstrably wrong. If so, admit it and get on with the interview.

15) Do not dwell at length on your present job

The opening question may relate to your present assignment. Answer the question but do not go into an extended discussion. You are being examined for a *new* job, not your present one. As a matter of fact, try to phrase ALL your answers in terms of the job for which you are being examined.

Basis of Rating

Probably you will forget most of these "do's" and "don'ts" when you walk into the oral interview room. Even remembering them all will not ensure you a passing grade. Perhaps you did not have the qualifications in the first place. But remembering them will help you to put your best foot forward, without treading on the toes of the board members.

Rumor and popular opinion to the contrary notwithstanding, an oral board wants you to make the best appearance possible. They know you are under pressure – but they also want to see how you respond to it as a guide to what your reaction would be under the pressures of the job you seek. They will be influenced by the degree of poise you display, the personal traits you show and the manner in which you respond.

ABOUT THIS BOOK

This book contains tests divided into Examination Sections. Go through each test, answering every question in the margin. At the end of each test look at the answer key and check your answers. On the ones you got wrong, look at the right answer choice and learn. Do not fill in the answers first. Do not memorize the questions and answers, but understand the answer and principles involved. On your test, the questions will likely be different from the samples. Questions are changed and new ones added. If you understand these past questions you should have success with any changes that arise. Tests may consist of several types of questions. We have additional books on each subject should more study be advisable or necessary for you. Finally, the more you study, the better prepared you will be. This book is intended to be the last thing you study before you walk into the examination room. Prior study of relevant texts is also recommended. NLC publishes some of these in our Fundamental Series. Knowledge and good sense are important factors in passing your exam. Good luck also helps. So now study this Passbook, absorb the material contained within and take that knowledge into the examination. Then do your best to pass that exam.

———

EXAMINATION SECTION

EXAMINATION SECTION
TEST 1

DIRECTIONS: Each question or incomplete statement is followed by several suggested answers or completions. Select the one that BEST answers the question or completes the statement. *PRINT THE LETTER OF THE CORRECT ANSWER IN THE SPACE AT THE RIGHT.*

1. The best example of positive transfer of learning is   1.____

   A. overhand throwing using a 2-inch foam ball and underhand throwing using a soft-ball
   B. striking a ball using a forehand tennis stroke and striking a ball using a forehand racquetball stroke
   C. throwing at a stationary target and throwing at a moving target
   D. walking in general space and skipping to music

2. The most effective type of practice after students experience a motor activity for the first time is   2.____

   A. distributed
   B. intermittent
   C. isolated
   D. massed

3. For students having difficulty in balancing on different body parts in an inverted position, the appropriate application of the mechanical principle of equilibrium is to   3.____

   A. decrease the size of the base of support
   B. increase the acceleration in establishing the position
   C. increase the size of the base of support
   D. move the vertical line of gravity to a position outside the base of support

4. When progressing in a striking skill from the use of the hand to the use of an implement (bat, racquet, stick), increasing the length of the lever will result in a/an   4.____

   A. decrease in force
   B. decrease in range of motion at the joint
   C. increase in force
   D. increase in speed of the lever

5. The most appropriate technique for a teacher to use while scanning to observe the performance of an entire class in scattered formation on a field is to   5.____

   A. focus on one child at a time
   B. focus on the highly skilled children
   C. maintain a position in the middle of the area
   D. move around the outside edge of the teaching area

6. In the development of proper throwing patterns, which sequence of tasks would be most appropriate?   6.____

A. tossing to a stationary partner; tossing to self; tossing to a moving partner; tossing while moving to a moving partner

B. tossing to a stationary partner; tossing to self; tossing while moving to a moving partner; throwing to a distant target

C. tossing to self; tossing to a moving partner; tossing to a stationary partner; throwing to a distant target

D. tossing to self; tossing to a stationary partner; tossing to a moving partner; tossing while moving to a moving partner

7. An 11-year-old boy taking the AAHPERD Skills Test in softball scores in the 55th percentile on the throw for distance test. This score indicates that the student's ability to throw is equal to the ability of

7.____

A. 45% of all boys his age in the test sample
B. 55% of all boys his age in the test sample
C. 55% of his male classmates
D. 55% of the average boys and girls his age

8. To develop manipulative skills in primary grade children, the teacher should provide each child with

8.____

A. equipment of any weight and any size
B. lightweight and/or short equipment
C. long implements and limited space
D. unlimited space and regulation-sized equipment

9. A teacher is planning an introductory lesson to develop a mature kicking pattern with fourth-grade children. There are 20 various sized balls, 16 children and a large grass area that includes a rebound wall and a fence. The most effective arrangement for optimum student learning of the kick is to

9.____

A. allow each child to choose a ball and practice kicking against a rebound wall or fence
B. group children in fours to play a game of circle dodgeball using kicking skills
C. group children in fours to play a modified game of soccer
D. have the children select partners, make choices of balls and practice kicking against a wall or fence

10. A seventh-grade class is playing a modified game of basketball in which the focus is on good defensive positioning and intercepting the ball. Which is the most effective defensive technique to employ?

10.____

A. Capitalize on opportunities to double-team the opposing passer
B. Continue to position the body between the guarded player and the goal
C. Focus eyes on the guarded player's pelvic area
D. Switch often from one-on-one to zone defense

2

11. A teacher working with fourth-grade students is planning a series of lessons designed to   11._____
teach students to play a modified game of soccer. Which is the most appropriate progression?

    A. Administer soccer skills test, practice individual skills and play a game of modified soccer
    B. Practice individual skills, combine skills and apply skills in a game-like setting
    C. Practice skills in a game-like setting, play a modified game of soccer and administer soccer skills test
    D. Play a modified game of soccer, practice weakest individual skills and replay a modified game of soccer

12. What are the best procedures for enhancing the safety of students in physical education   12._____
classes?
    I. Have equipment ready and in place when students report to class
    II. Restrict the use of climbing equipment unless the teacher is present to spot
    III. Review rules for use of equipment before students participate in an activity
    IV. Stop off-task behavior immediately, before it spreads

    A. II and III
    B. I and II
    C. I, III and IV
    D. I, II, III and IV

13. What is the most important consideration when designing a new playground?   13._____

    A. A plan for single-task involvement play areas
    B. The developmental needs of students
    C. The placement of permanent equipment to facilitate supervision
    D. The morphological development of students

14. A systematic increase in the level of exercise needed to improve physical fitness is   14._____

    A. frequency
    B. progression
    C. specificity
    D. target training

15. Based on his scores, what type of program would be advisable for a 130-pound eighth-   15._____
grade boy who scored at the 90th percentile on body composition and at the 40th percentile on cardiovascular endurance?

    A. A jogging program to increase cardiovascular endurance
    B. A low-calorie diet to reduce body fat
    C. A weight training program to increase lean weight and decrease fat weight
    D. Ballistic stretching to increase cardiovascular endurance

16. The results of the AAHPERD sit-and-reach fitness test indicate that a student is lacking   16._____
in the component of flexibility. The teacher should recommend

    A. a daily routine of static stretching exercises
    B. alternate ballistic and static stretching
    C. ballistic stretching 3 to 4 times a week for 20 minutes
    D. low impact aerobic activities once a week

17. The results of a fitness test show that students in a first-grade class need improvement in upper body strength. What would be an appropriate activity to improve this component?   17.____

    A. Push-ups
    B. Seal walk
    C. Tug-of-war
    D. Weightlifting

18. Of the following, the most accurate instrument to measure body composition is a   18.____

    A. balanced scale
    B. dynamometer
    C. skinfold caliper
    D. tape measure

19. Fifth-grade students taking the AAHPERD Fitness Test performed poorly in the muscular strength and endurance items. If curl-ups are used to improve the students' performance in this area, which technique would be most appropriate?   19.____

    A. Bent-knee curl-ups with each hand on the opposite shoulder
    B. Bent-knee curl-ups with the hands behind the head
    C. Straight-legged curl-ups with each hand on the opposite shoulder
    D. Straight-legged curl-ups with the hand behind the head

---

KEY (CORRECT ANSWERS)

1.	C		11.	B
2.	A		12.	D
3.	C		13.	B
4.	C		14.	B
5.	D		15.	A
6.	D		16.	A
7.	B		17.	B
8.	B		18.	C
9.	A		19.	A
10.	B			

EXAMINATION SECTION
TEST 1

DIRECTIONS: Each question or incomplete statement is followed by several suggested answers or completions. Select the one that BEST answers the question or completes the statement. *PRINT THE LETTER OF THE CORRECT ANSWER IN THE SPACE AT THE RIGHT.*

1. During long periods of exercise without rehydration, fluid redistribution in the body and loss of fluids due to sweating can lead to   1._____

    A. decreased heart rate
    B. lowered body temperature
    C. reduced blood plasma volume
    D. decreased gas exchange between alveoli and capillaries

2. Which of the following statements is an accurate interpretation of the FITT (frequency, intensity, time, type) principle as applied to flexibility training?   2._____

    A. Frequency refers to how long a stretch is held multiplied by the number of times the stretch is performed
    B. Intensity refers to the principle that to increase flexibility, one must stretch until one feels intense pressure in muscles and joints
    C. Time refers to the principle that to elongate muscle and connective tissue, one must stretch with quick, pulsing movements
    D. Type refers to the mode of exercise suitable to the purpose of training; for example, to increase arm and shoulder flexibility, one must stretch arm and shoulder muscles and joints

3. Which of the following best describes the main physiological principle underlying the importance of aerobic conditioning for cardiorespiratory fitness?   3._____

    A. Aerobic exercise leads to lowered resting metabolism rates, which improves cardiorespiratory functioning
    B. Aerobic exercise increases flexibility, and a flexible body can better tolerate cardiorespiratory endurance activities
    C. The circulatory system-the systemic arteries and veins-relies on exercise to trigger the process of circulating oxygen-rich blood to organs
    D. The heart and lungs act like muscles: the more they are exercised-contracted and released-the more efficiently they work

4. During a high school weight-bearing activities unit, a few students perform standing lifts with weighted bars and barbells incorrectly. The lifts are too rapid and jerky. The most important reason to avoid lifting with excessive speed or with jerky motions is that these practices   4._____

    A. force the back into an upright position, which should be arched slowly during a lift
    B. cause side bending and twisting, resulting in lateral flexion of muscles
    C. dramatically increase pressure on the spine and tension in the spinal muscles
    D. significantly increase momentum, nearly eliminating the work being done by muscles

5. During a fitness class focusing on posture, students make up slogans to promote proper form for standing. Which of the following student slogans reflects an accurate understanding of the body mechanics involved in proper posture?

    A. "To make sure you stand with back aligned, put your ears, shoulders and hips in a straight line."
    B. "Let your spine flex when you stand, to keep back and neck in line."
    C. "Extend your upper body forward a slight way, to make sure you're standing the right way."
    D. "Stand with your weight toward the back of your body, to decrease the load on the front of your body."

5.____

6. Which of the following best explains the role of regular muscular strength training in improving body composition?

    A. Strength training can target specific areas of body fat and change fat into muscle through exercises for that part of the body
    B. Muscular strength training (e.g., weight lifting) burns more calories than aerobic training
    C. Strength training builds and preserves lean muscle tissue, which uses more calories at rest than fat tissue uses at rest
    D. Muscular strength training allows participants to "bulk up" quickly

6.____

7. A ninth-grade student who is moderately fit is beginning an individual fitness program. He enjoys the outdoors so he plans to bike, jog and cross-country ski. Which of the following is the most appropriate guideline for this student to incorporate into his fitness program at this time?

    A. Exercise at an intensity of 60 to 75 percent of maximum heart rate
    B. Exercise for 20 minutes three times a week
    C. Exercise at an intensity of 75 to 90 percent of maximum heart rate
    D. Exercise for 90 minutes each day of the week

7.____

8. During an outdoor physical education class, small groups of middle school students practice the following set of movements with rubber balls:
Throw the ball as far as you can:
    1. using wrist motion only
    2. using wrist and elbow motion, but with arm stationary
    3. using wrist, elbow and shoulder motion, but with trunk stationary
    4. using entire arm, with trunk rotation
Which of the following biomechanical concepts is illustrated by these activities?

    A. Flow is the ability to combine movements smoothly, even when varying balance, pathway or speed
    B. The force generated by a moving body increases with the range of motion and number of involved body segments
    C. The optimal angle of release for throwing a ball for maximum distance is 45 degrees
    D. Coordination of motion involves a sequential progression of motions beginning with the more proximal body segments and ending with the more distal segments

8.____

9. Which of the following statements reflects an accurate understanding of a basic principle   9._____
    of motor development?

    A. Among children, motor skills generally appear automatically and develop at
        approximately the same rate
    B. Motor development is most related to educational level, e.g., most fifth graders will
        exhibit about the same level of motor skill development
    C. Individuals reach large-motor skill milestones (e.g. walking, running, jumping) at
        the same age, but differ dramatically in fine-motor skill development
    D. Motor development occurs differently in individuals, and progressive developmen-
        tal changes do not happen automatically with maturation

10. Which of the following is the best analysis of the stage of motor development this student   10._____
    exhibits in performing the overhand throw?

    A. The child is in the initial stage of development because the throwing action is
        mainly from the elbow
    B. The child is in the elementary stage of development because the forward leg is on
        the same side as the throwing arm
    C. The child is in the mature stage of development because the throwing arm is
        swung backward in preparation of the throw
    D. The child is in the advanced stage of development because there is a definite rota-
        tion through the hips, legs, spine and shoulders during the throw

11. Pairs of high school physical education students practice the overhand throw with foam   11._____
    balls, concentrating on the form and technique involved in the throwing pattern. Later, the
    teacher shows students several other sports movements that use this motor pattern.
    Which of the following uses the same motor pattern as the overhand throw?

    A. Forehand drive in tennis
    B. Backhand throw in Frisbee golf
    C. Forward pass in football
    D. Propelling in cross-country skiing

12. In softball, which position would best prepare an infielder to move quickly in any direction   12._____
    when reacting to a batted ball? The body

    A. held erect with the feet placed well apart
    B. bent forward with the feet placed well apart

C. held erect with the feet close together
D. bent forward with the feet close together

13. When beginning a unit on self-defense with middle school students, which of the follow- 13.____
ing activities should take place *first?*

    A. Have students choose one type of martial art and write a short, informative report on it
    B. Ask students who have taken self-defense lessons to demonstrate what they have learned for the class
    C. Demonstrate and describe the self-defense stance, correct breathing technique, the stomp, the knee kick, the front snap kick and the side kick
    D. Discuss safety procedures such as assessing possible risks in a situation, staying alert, walking purposefully, not hitchhiking and staying lighted areas

Questions 14 and 15 refer to the following statement:

In a first-grade physical education class, students use multicolored streamers with handles called "rainbow ribbons" to trace the shapes of letters in the air. As each letter is announced, students "draw" it in the air using their rainbow ribbons.

14. Which of the following best describes the role of integrated learning in this activity? 14.____

    A. Students are exploring levels such as high, medium and low by drawing the letters in the air at different heights
    B. Academic content is being reinforced through kinesthetic learning; students feel the shapes of letters through movement
    C. Spatial concepts such as up, down, forward, backward and sideways are being reinforced through direct teaching of the alphabet
    D. Students are exploring pathways by making the letters while traveling in different locomotor patterns

15. After the alphabet letters, the teacher asks students to try the "figure eight," the "rattle- 15.____
snake" and the "tornado," all of which the teacher demonstrates. Which of the following additions to this lesson would bets promote student creativity in the context of physical activity?

    A. Asking students to draw geometric shapes such as circles, ovals, squares and tri-angles in the air with the streamers
    B. Putting on music and asking students to mimic the teacher's movements in time to the rhythms they hear
    C. Challenging students to play a follow-the-leader type game with the streamers waving and twirling
    D. Challenging students to make up their own shapes or movements with the stream-ers

16. A physical education teacher knows that many of his students cycle, skateboard and roll-erblade. The teacher wants to emphasize to students that safety helmets are good investments that provide important benefits. Which of the following is appropriate consumer-oriented advice to pass along to students?

    A. Polystyrene (foam-lined) helmets are a good choice because they are inexpensive, impact resistant and conform to safety standards
    B. Cost is a gauge of quality. More expensive helmets always provide better protection than inexpensive ones.
    C. Choose from among the newest, more expensive styles of helmets because they are more likely to conform to safety standards
    D. Regardless of price, helmets that do not cover the ears are better than full helmets because they permit more hearing

16.____

17. Many high schools offer nontraditional physical education courses such as line dancing, rock climbing, tai chi, juggling, backpacking, field archery, snowboarding and yoga. Which of the following is the primary purpose for including diverse courses in a secondary physical education curriculum?

    A. Enable the teaching of decision-making and problem-solving skills in all secondary physical education activities
    B. Increase student awareness of recreational opportunities that are inexpensive and available throughout the year
    C. Attract students to physical education and spark long-term interest and participation in physical activity
    D. Offer the latest adventure sports so that physical education classes will gain the support of parents and community members

17.____

18. During a racquet skills unit, a sixth-grade student with a learning disability needs a few minutes of extra time for transitions between activity stations. Which of the following practices would be most appropriate to use in addressing this situation?

    A. Agree upon a strategy, such as a hand signal from the teacher, that alerts the student to prepare for upcoming transitions
    B. Assign a small group of student "buddies" to rotate through the station activities with the student at the student's own pace
    C. Take the student out of the activity several minutes early and bring the student to a new station before the other students change activities
    D. Allow the student to finish activities after the other students, then escort the student to new activities

18.____

19. In a secondary physical education class, students practice free throws at the end of each class during a unit on basketball. Students take turns videotaping one another as they practice their shots. The videotape is available later in the physical education office for students to view. The primary advantage of this assessment strategy is that it

    A. allows students to easily compare their performance with the performance of peers
    B. provides documentation that the physical education program uses authentic performance assessment

19.____

9

C. allows students to analyze their shots and determine ways to improve their performance
D. provides a strong indication of whether students understand the movement concepts underlying the sport skill

20. Which of the following statements best describes the general impact that Title IX of the Educational Amendments has had on women's sports since it was enacted in 1972?   20.____

    A. Its mandate that colleges and universities initiate women's sports enhancement programs has resulted in equal numbers of female and male teams
    B. Women have attained approximately the same level of participation in NCAA sports as men
    C. High school female athletes have received athletic scholarships as frequently and in the same amounts as their male counterparts
    D. Women and girls have benefited greatly from increased access to teams, facilities, equipment and schedules in school athletic programs

21. Sid is a 14-year-old boy with asthma who lives in the city. He enjoys exercising outdoors, and often bicycles in good weather to get places. Which of the following strategies would best minimize Sid's exposure to smog while exercising outdoors?   21.____

    A. Exercise before 10 a.m. whenever possible
    B. Exercise in the evening rather than during the day
    C. Increase intensity of exercise and decrease duration
    D. Exercise in a sheltered area rather than in an open area

22. Within the human movement sciences and education field, college graduates with degrees in health promotion are likely to be most prepared to find employment as   22.____

    A. managers of sports and leisure facilities and events
    B. sports medicine consultants to colleges and universities and to professional athletes and teams
    C. athletic directors of schools, municipal parks, youth clubs and recreation departments
    D. wellness professionals in health centers, nursing homes, retirement communities and public agencies

KEY (CORRECT ANSWERS)

1.	C		11.	C
2.	D		12.	B
3.	D		13.	D
4.	C		14.	B
5.	A		15.	D
6.	C		16.	A
7.	A		17.	C
8.	B		18.	A
9.	D		19.	C
10.	B		20.	D

21.	A
22.	D

EXAMINATION SECTION
TEST 1

DIRECTIONS: Each question or incomplete statement is followed by several suggested answers or completions. Select the one that BEST answers the question or completes the statement. *PRINT THE LETTER OF THE CORRECT ANSWER IN THE SPACE AT THE RIGHT.*

1. According to contemporary thought, each of the following is a general function of sport in society EXCEPT as a(n)   1._____

    A.   agent of change
    B.   establisher of collective conscience
    C.   emotional release mechanism
    D.   producer of diversity and multiperspective

2. A person's hematocrit is a measure of the relative amount of _____ in blood.   2._____

    A.   amino acids and fats   B.   plasma and corpuscles
    C.   water and oxygen   D.   proteins and antibodies

3. Being asked to dribble toward a basket, stop, and shoot, is an example of a(n) _____ game skill experience.   3._____

    A.   invariant   B.   dynamic   C.   playing   D.   static

4. Each of the following is a purpose of dance experiences in physical education EXCEPT   4._____

    A.   the ability to perform rhythmic dance movements in a competitive setting
    B.   the ability to use the body to express feelings and attitudes
    C.   the ability to interpret and move to different rhythms
    D.   enjoyment and appreciation of dance as a worthwhile experience for all

5. The development of physical education as a series of light exercises designed to prevent disease appears to have been first introduced in   5._____

    A.   China   B.   Sweden   C.   Greece   D.   India

6. What area of study is specifically concerned with time and space factors in the motion of a system?   6._____

    A.   Kinesthetics   B.   Kinesiology
    C.   Kinetics   D.   Kinematics

7. For maximum clarity, a teacher's message about a student's performed movement should contain each of the following EXCEPT a   7._____

    A.   single suggestion as to what the student can practice in order to improve proficiency
    B.   contrast between the observed performance and the desired performance
    C.   contrast between the observed performance and the performance of other students in the same age group
    D.   brief description of what the teacher observed

8. Which of the following is an educational objective written for the affective domain? Students will be able to

    A. dribble a ball successfully from one end of the court to another while maintaining a moderate pace
    B. dive, using good form, from a three-meter diving board
    C. work quietly and on task while sharing equipment with others
    D. explain why maintaining a lower position, with the knees bent, allows them to better defend against opponents

8._____

9. Which of the following is NOT an element of the functional-aggression hypothesis? The

    A. inhibition of direct acts of aggression is an additional frustration that instigates aggression against the agent perceived to be responsible for this inhibition
    B. strongest instigation aroused by frustration is to direct acts of inhibition of the aggressor's behavior
    C. expression of any act of aggression is a catharsis that reduces the instigation to all other acts of aggression
    D. inhibition of any act of aggression varies directly with the strength of the punishment anticipated for its expression

9._____

10. Beginning in the 1950s, American physical education began to de-emphasize

    A. growth and development
    B. nutrition and weight control
    C. the systems of the body
    D. mental health

10._____

11. Which of the following is not a category of movement typically used in physical education applications?

    A. Locomotion
    B. Articulation
    C. Manipulation
    D. Stability

11._____

12. In a(n) _____ nerve cell, a single process connects both the axon and the dendrite to the cell body, and the dendrite takes on all the characteristics of the axon.

    A. non-polar
    B. unipolar
    C. bipolar
    D. multipolar

12._____

13. The principal limiting factor for most types of exercise that lasts longer than three or four minutes is

    A. lung capacity
    B. the capacity to deliver oxygen to working muscles
    C. maximum systolic blood pressure
    D. the maximum heart rate

13._____

14. Which of the following would LEAST affect a student's growth and development?

    A. Nutrition
    B. Genetic factors
    C. Social factors
    D. Activity

14._____

15. For a group of students to acquire motor behaviors, the MOST desirable method is to arrange groups by   15.____

    A. gender   B. interest   C. chance   D. ability

16. Which of the following is a DISADVANTAGE associated with isotonic exercises?   16.____

    A. Use of only concentric contractions
    B. Muscle soreness
    C. Provide erratic resistance for muscle contractions
    D. Progress cannot be objectively measured

17. Each of the following is an objective for health education established by the NEA and the AMA's joint commission EXCEPT to   17.____

    A. promote satisfactory ways of behaving among parents and adults so that they may maintain and improve the health of the home and community
    B. instruct children and young people so that they may conserve and improve their own health
    C. improve the individual and community life of the future
    D. create opportunities for personal expression and creative experiences as an antidote to materialism

18. Any muscle other than the prime mover that acts to aid, support, or guide the action caused by the prime mover is known as a(n)   18.____

    A. fixator   B. synergist
    C. auxiliary   D. extensor

19. An effective development goal for physical education is to   19.____

    A. foster an environment that will encourage children to be multisensory learners
    B. assist children in becoming positive, self-discovering learners
    C. provide children with opportunities to become fit movers
    D. aid children in becoming knowledgeable movers

20. A person with a stocky, muscular body build is known as a(n)   20.____

    A. ectomorph   B. endomorph
    C. mesomorph   D. somatomorph

21. Which of the following statements is FALSE?   21.____

    A. Health and physical fitness are separate and distinct characteristics, but can limit each other.
    B. Levels of physical fitness can only be defined in terms of a given individual.
    C. Exceptional motor ability is typically a prerequisite for the attainment of high levels of physical fitness.
    D. Any reasonably healthy person can achieve vast improvement in his/her physical fitness.

22. The establishment of professional physical education objectives is sometimes simplified   22.____
by selecting objectives on the basis of the uniqueness of the contributions of physical
education to individuals.
The MAIN problem with this approach is that

   A. it encourages conformity
   B. the relative importance of possible objectives is ignored
   C. there can be no continuity within a school's curriculum
   D. it often produces educators who are indifferent to social norms

23. Each of the following is a training factor which can be adjusted in order to accomplish   23.____
overload EXCEPT

   A. response rate   B. frequency
   C. duration   D. intensity

24. During heavy exercise, a person's heart rate typically   24.____

   A. doubles   B. triples
   C. quadruples   D. is increased five times

25. Which of the following terms is used as a description of a level of total fitness?   25.____

   A. Subminimal   B. Minimal
   C. Suboptimal   D. Optimal

KEY (CORRECT ANSWERS)

1.	D	11.	B
2.	B	12.	B
3.	B	13.	B
4.	A	14.	C
5.	A	15.	D
6.	D	16.	B
7.	C	17.	D
8.	C	18.	B
9.	B	19.	B
10.	C	20.	C

21.	C
22.	B
23.	A
24.	B
25.	C

TEST 2

DIRECTIONS: Each question or incomplete statement is followed by several suggested answers or completions. Select the one that BEST answers the question or completes the statement. *PRINT THE LETTER OF THE CORRECT ANSWER IN THE SPACE AT THE RIGHT.*

1. Generally, what type of competition is emphasized by societies that stress responsibility training?   1._____

   A. Games of physical skill   B. Puzzles
   C. Games of chance   D. Games of strategy

2. In the years immediately following World War I, American physical education focused primarily on   2._____

   A. health   B. preparedness
   C. social adjustment   D. fitness

3. Each of the following is a basic format element of a unit plan EXCEPT   3._____

   A. block time plan for the unit
   B. evaluation procedures
   C. developmental analysis
   D. an identification of the sequence and scope of content

4. In 1840, the American educator _____ emphasized the importance of physical well-being and *educating for health.*   4._____

   A. John Dewey   B. Jerome Bruner
   C. Theodore Sizer   D. Horace Mann

5. Which of the following statements is FALSE?   5._____

   A. The boundaries of the discipline of physical education cannot be adequately defined in terms of what its practitioners do.
   B. As a concept, health means simply the absence of disease.
   C. The possibility of mass leisure is as much a threat as a blessing to any society,
   D. The fact that a given professional objective has widespread support does not mean that it is more important than other less popular objectives.

6. An educational outcome specified for the development of feelings, attitudes, values, and/or social behaviors is described as a(n) _____ objective.   6._____

   A. affective   B. demonstrative
   C. psychomotor   D. cognitive

7. Which of the following is NOT an important characteristic of a good behavioral objective?   7._____

   A. Measurability
   B. Adjustability
   C. Observability
   D. They establish criteria for performance

8. What is the term for the improvement of a skill over a period of nonpractice?   8._____

    A. Atrophy
    C. Extension
    B. Reminiscence
    D. Macropassage

9. A student who is able to perform inverted balances has achieved the _____ level of bal-   9._____
   ancing skill acquisition.

    A. precontrol
    C. utilization
    B. control
    D. proficiency

10. Perceptual-motor tests may be used by physical educators to evaluate each of the follow-   10._____
    ing EXCEPT

    A. peripheral vision
    C. agility
    B. hand-eye coordination
    D. visual acuity

11. Which of the following is NOT an issue currently affecting the health and fitness of Amer-   11._____
    icans?

    A. Decreased leisure time
    B. Increased life span
    C. Regulation of drugs and food additives
    D. The effects of stress

12. Strength differences that exist between the sexes are primarily the result of differences in   12._____

    A. attitude
    B. isotonic training
    C. time spent exercising muscles
    D. muscle mass

13. Deoxygenated blood enters the heart at the   13._____

    A. right ventricle
    C. right atrium
    B. left ventricle
    D. left atrium

14. Each of the following is a component part of an educational objective EXCEPT   14._____

    A. performance level expected
    B. expected behavior
    C. evaluation system used
    D. condition under which behavior is to be exhibited

15. At around the time of _____, the average American citizen began to develop an under-   15._____
    standing and appreciation of leisure.

    A. early twentieth-century immigration explosions
    B. the Industrial Revolution
    C. the Baby Boom
    D. World War I

16. The first archeological evidence of ball games was discovered in   16._____

    A. Egypt
    C. North America
    B. China
    D. India

17. Which of the following is NOT a cardiovascular or respiratory change associated with a regular program of exercise?

    17._____

    A. Increase in heart size
    B. Reduction in cardiac output during submaximal exercise
    C. Reduction in blood plasma volume
    D. Increase in maximum cardiac output

18. The ratio of force required to overcome friction between two surfaces to the normal force pressing the surfaces together, when one surface is sliding over the other at a constant speed, is known as _____ friction.

    18._____

    A. static   B. rolling   C. fluid   D. kinetic

19. In the pre-adolescent stage of development, some students do not enter fully into the play involved in a physical education program. Each of the following tends to be a cultural characteristic imposed on these students EXCEPT

    19._____

    A. they are considered by boys and girls to be much less able to fulfill school positions demanding virtue
    B. they tend to exhibit negative behaviors
    C. they are less socially acceptable to other boys and girls
    D. they tend to regard others as less acceptable than they are regarded by other boys and girls

20. A force directed perpendicular to an object is described as

    20._____

    A. resistive   B. normal   C. axial   D. opposite

21. The facts and concepts of human growth and development are important to the physical educator for each of the following reasons EXCEPT they

    21._____

    A. provide a basis for recognizing deviations from existing patterns
    B. enable a teacher to help the persons involved to understand themselves
    C. provide a framework for grading and evaluation
    D. provide a sound basis for program planning

22. At the utilization level of skill acquisition, a rhythmic At the utilization level of skill acquisition, a rhythmic dance experience is MOST likely to involve

    22._____

    A. repeating movements to a varying rhythm
    B. performing a variety of movements while focusing on extraneous, outside factors
    C. remembering a sequence of movements that are to be performed to a rhythm
    D. guiding the creation of simple sequences

23. Which of the following is an informal method of evaluating student performance?

    23._____

    A. Skills tests   B. Records of performance
    C. Rating scales   D. Written test

24. Which of the following is a characteristic of the control level of a student's skill proficiency?

    A. Movement can still be performed successfully even when the context of the task is varied.
    B. The child is unable to repeat movements in succession.
    C. The skill has become automatic.
    D. Movements are more consistent in appearance and repetitions are somewhat alike.

24.____

25. What is the term for the length of time a given intensity of muscle contraction can be maintained?

    A. Static muscular endurance
    B. Dynamic muscular endurance
    C. Static strength
    D. Dynamic strength

25.____

KEY (CORRECT ANSWERS)

1.	C	11.	A
2.	B	12.	D
3.	C	13.	C
4.	D	14.	C
5.	B	15.	B
6.	A	16.	A
7.	B	17.	C
8.	B	18.	D
9.	B	19.	D
10.	C	20.	B

21.	C
22.	B
23.	C
24.	D
25.	A

TEST 3

DIRECTIONS: Each question or incomplete statement is followed by several suggested answers or completions. Select the one that BEST answers the question or completes the statement. *PRINT THE LETTER OF THE CORRECT ANSWER IN THE SPACE AT THE RIGHT.*

1. Each of the following is an association within the parent group AAHPERD EXCEPT

    A. American Association for Leisure and Recreation
    B. National Dance Association
    C. National Intramural-Recreational Sports Association
    D. Association for the Advancement of Health Education

1.____

2. A long-distance runner is 17 years old. Her resting heart rate is 100. What would be her optimal training heart rate?

    A. 150   B. 162   C. 187   D. 203

2.____

3. Which of the following is NOT an objective established by the Commission on Goals for American Recreation?

    A. Democratic human relations
    B. Effective and appropriate health skills
    C. Leisure skills and interest
    D. Personal fulfillment

3.____

4. Within the sphere of physical education, the philosophy of rationalism most strongly influenced the

    A. athletic ideal of ancient Greece
    B. post-World War II teachings of Ludwig Klages
    C. functional movements of twentieth-century America
    D. nineteenth-century *Turn* movement of German formal exercise

4.____

5. Qualities are classified as components of physical fitness if they

    A. can be quantitatively measured
    B. are essential to health and/or work capacity
    C. have at least some relation to cardio-respiratory functions
    D. are essential to skill and motor performance

5.____

6. When peer teaching experiences are used for one or more instructional components of a physical education program, the

    A. teacher's emphasis shifts from the performance of the learner to guiding the peer relationship
    B. peer teacher typically teaches for most of a class period
    C. peer teacher assumes the entire responsibility for content transmission
    D. structure of learning experiences is decided upon by peer teachers

6.____

7. Which of the following is NOT a quality of white muscle fibers?

    A. Larger size   B. Suited to high-intensity work
    C. Aerobic orientation   D. More forceful

7.____

8. Which of the following is an educational objective written for the cognitive domain?   8.____
Students will be able to

    A. describe how force is produced in overhand throwing patterns
    B. pass a ball accurately from at least 15 yards to a moving player in a game situation
    C. work cooperatively in pairs while learning individual tumbling moves
    D. describe why their hearts beat faster during hard exercise

9. The _____ plane divides the human body into a right half and a left half.   9.____

    A. frontal   B. temporal
    C. transverse   D. sagittal

10. Most often, _____ skills are emphasized in an American physical education program.   10.____

    A. interpretive   B. social
    C. expressive   D. sports

11. According to the philosophical theories of _____, physical activity is held in high esteem   11.____
if it contributes to the development of some of the enduring virtues such as self-discipline
and courage.

    A. existentialism   B. pragmatism
    C. idealism   D. realism

12. Competitive situations tend to impair motor performance of   12.____

    A. tasks involving strength
    B. complex tasks
    C. tasks involving muscular endurance
    D. simple skills

13. Which of the following is not a helpful strategy for implementing a physical education les-   13.____
son?

    A. Begin class with a vigorous warm-up activity focusing on the fitness strand of the
        lesson
    B. Emphasize body mechanics prior to the result
    C. Evaluate each lesson in terms of achievement of objectives
    D. Be certain to incorporate the cognitive and affective strands into the lesson sepa-
        rately and at different times

14. Cardiac output is a product of   14.____

    A. heart rate and systemic arterial pressure
    B. filling pressure and diastole
    C. stroke volume and contractility
    D. heart rate and stroke volume

15. A person's physical strength has been positively linked to each of the following social   15.____
characteristics EXCEPT

    A. leadership   B. behavior
    C. social status   D. adjustment

16. The behavioral component of a learner's attitude is formed by 16.____

    A. the categorization of events occurring in the environment
    B. social norms
    C. stereotyping
    D. association of physiological responses with certain cognitions

17. The amount of air remaining in the lungs at the end of maximal expiration is known as 17.____

    A. tidal volume   B. expiratory reserve volume
    C. residual volume   D. total lung capacity

18. During the instructional process, there are several basic ways in which physical educa- 18.____
tion teachers can provide students within the content dimension of the task through design.
Presentation of _____ is NOT one of these.

    A. verbal problems solvable only through verbal responses
    B. alternative conditions of performance
    C. tasks with multiple correct responses
    D. alternative tasks

19. The ability to start, stop, and change directions quickly is known as 19.____

    A. coordination   B. agility
    C. motility   D. dexterity

20. Which of the following statements about punishment as a behavior-altering response is 20.____
true?
Punishment('s)

    A. does not significantly alter behavior
    B. does alter behavior, but its effects tend to be less permanent than reward
    C. will never lead to an increase in the undesirable behavior
    D. effect is equal to, but opposite, the effect of reward

21. A typical diastolic blood pressure for a young adult female would be 21.____

    A. 70   B. 85   C. 110   D. 125

22. Raising the arms to the side is an example of 22.____

    A. abduction   B. adduction
    C. pronation   D. flexion

23. The use of demonstration as a teaching tool in physical education should be guided by 23.____
each of the following principles EXCEPT

    A. student demonstrations are preferable to teacher demonstrations
    B. demonstrations should help explain why a skill is performed in a certain way
    C. student practice of demonstrated skills should occur immediately after a given demonstration
    D. demonstrations should use an organizational format similar to the skill being demonstrated

24. In situations where muscle contracts and maintains tension while lengthening against resistance such as gravity, the contraction is described as   24.____

    A. static   B. concentric
    C. kinetic   D. eccentric

25. Which of the following is an area of knowledge that is currently of little importance in professional physical education programs?   25.____

    A. Mathematics   B. Philosophy
    C. Fine arts   D. Psychology

KEY (CORRECT ANSWERS)

1.	C		11.	C
2.	B		12.	B
3.	B		13.	D
4.	D		14.	D
5.	B		15.	A
6.	A		16.	B
7.	C		17.	C
8.	A		18.	A
9.	D		19.	B
10.	D		20.	B

21. A
22. A
23. C
24. D
25. C

TEST 4

DIRECTIONS: Each question or incomplete statement is followed by several suggested answers or completions. Select the one that BEST answers the question or completes the statement. *PRINT THE LETTER OF THE CORRECT ANSWER IN THE SPACE AT THE RIGHT.*

1. Which of the following is a weakness most commonly associated with the use of interactive teaching strategies in physical education?

    A. Difficult to individualize content
    B. Progression of instruction is often too rigid
    C. Difficulty in feedback and evaluation
    D. Difficulty in adjusting communication

    1.____

2. Which of the following student behaviors lies within the *affective* domain?

    A. Response
    C. Evaluation
    B. Analysis
    D. Comprehension

    2.____

3. According to most definitions, each of the following is a characteristic of play EXCEPT it

    A. is free of the limitations of time
    B. is related to activities in which a person normally participates
    C. has no utilitarian value
    D. is begun and ended at will

    3.____

4. Which of the following is considered to be an element of motor fitness?

    A. Agility
    C. Perception
    B. Reflexes
    D. Motor response

    4.____

5. An example of an invariant game skill experience is

    A. defending against a sideline throw-in during a simulated soccer experience
    B. kicking a ball past a defender into a goal
    C. taking a ball away from an offensive player who is trying to score a goal
    D. kicking a ball at a target from behind a designated line

    5.____

6. Which of the following is a term for a reduction in muscle size?

    A. Edema
    C. Cyanosis
    B. Atrophy
    D. Contractility

    6.____

7. At the most basic level, rhythmic dance experiences are used to

    A. create simple sequences of movement
    B. create an unconscious understanding of mathematical concepts in physical education
    C. expose inherent rhythms in some movements
    D. reinforce movement concepts and themes that are already being studied

    7.____

8. The triceps brachii causing elbow extension is an example of a(n)

    A. synergist
    C. antagonist
    B. agonist
    D. reflex

    8.____

9. The primary DISADVANTAGE associated with isokinetic training is   9.____

    A. accentuation of weakness points
    B. expense of requisite equipment
    C. muscle soreness
    D. limited resistance against contraction

10. Each of the following is a teacher function that is important to discriminating teaching   10.____
strategies EXCEPT

    A. progression of content
    B. provision for feedback and evaluation
    C. division of students by ability
    D. communication of tasks

11. What is the term for the change brought about by a student's experience?   11.____

    A. Learning   B. Development
    C. Maturity   D. Growth

12. A basketball team's members are presented with a set of plays to memorize. The plays   12.____
are printed in a playbook for each of the players, and during every practice, the instructor
has the team run through the plays in the order in which they appear in the playbook. The
team members seen to have greater trouble remembering the plays that appear toward
the middle of the playbook.
This is an illustration of

    A. pertinence theory
    B. the primacy-recency effect
    C. the filter theory
    D. long-term memory loss

13. The first professional organization in the area of American recreation was the   13.____

    A. National Recreation and Parks Association
    B. American Association for Leisure and Recreation
    C. AAHPERD
    D. National Playground Association

14. The ways in which physical activity affect a student's psychological factors are referred to   14.____
as _____ concepts.

    A. proprioceptive   B. efferent
    C. sensorimotor   D. afferent

15. Games of physical skill are most likely to be valued by societies which emphasize train-   15.____
ing in

    A. achievement   B. responsibility
    C. obedience   D. aesthetic appreciation

16. Which of the following is an application involving kinetic friction?   16.____

    A. An approach shot in golf
    B. The streamlining of a swimmer during practice

C. An attempt to pull a heavy mat across a floor
D. Basketball players slipping and falling during practice

17. Which of the following statements is FALSE?   17._____

    A. Observation by spectators does not tend to contribute to improvement of certain kinds of motor performance, and is usually a deterrent.
    B. Socially-based motives, as opposed to rational thought or logic, are most often found to be responsible for people's participation in physical activity.
    C. Motor capacity is affected by maturation and early experience in exploration of one's environment.
    D. Academic achievement will typically have a moderate positive relationship to physical fitness and motor scores.

18. Which of the following American educators struggled to reconcile the term *physical education* with the idea that the spheres of mental and physical activity were inseparable?   18._____

    A. Mann   B. Dewey   C. Bruner   D. Nash

19. During exercise, each of the following blood factors increases in content EXCEPT   19._____

    A. acidity   B. oxygen
    C. temperature   D. glucose

20. Which of the following weight transfer skills illustrates the proficiency level of skill acquisition?   20._____

    A. Transferring weight from feet to hands
    B. Dismounting apparatus from hands to feet
    C. Transferring weight to a partner
    D. Stretching, curling, and twisting beneath points of contact

21. Rapid muscular movements that are started by prime movers but are completed by their own momentum are described as _____ movements.   21._____

    A. ballistic   B. spasmodic
    C. isometric   D. agonistic

22. Which of the following would be considered a *curricular* objective?   22._____

    A. The student will be able to perform several defensive wrestling moves during a match situation.
    B. The student will be able to use the bunting technique to move a runner up one base in a game situation, with pitches that appear capable of being bunted.
    C. The student will be able to play one individual sport at an intermediate level of difficulty.
    D. Taking just one step, the student will be able to hit a backhand stroke with good form into the opponent's court from a tossed ball.

23. When the angle at a joint is *increased,* _____ occurs.   23._____

    A. pronation   B. extension
    C. abduction   D. flexion

24. High achievement motivation is generally associated with each of the following EXCEPT   24._____

    A. relatively late demands for accomplishment
    B. adult interest and involvement in a child's achievement endeavors
    C. affectively intense rewards for accomplishments
    D. relatively high goals set for children by parents

25. Which of the following is an example of anaerobic activity?   25._____

    A. Endurance swimming   B. Bicycling
    C. Sprinting   D. Water polo

———

KEY (CORRECT ANSWERS)

1.	C	11.	A
2.	A	12.	B
3.	B	13.	D
4.	A	14.	B
5.	D	15.	A
6.	B	16.	D
7.	D	17.	A
8.	C	18.	D
9.	B	19.	D
10.	C	20.	B

21.	A
22.	C
23.	B
24.	A
25.	C

———

EXAMINATION SECTION
TEST 1

DIRECTIONS: Each question or incomplete statement is followed by several suggested answers or completions. Select the one that BEST answers the question or completes the statement. *PRINT THE LETTER OF THE CORRECT ANSWER IN THE SPACE AT THE RIGHT.*

1. Of the following, the MOST desirable help that can be rendered by volunteer assistants in the playground program is in

    A. preparing materials
    B. making individual corrections
    C. teaching game skills
    D. inspecting for safety hazards

1.____

2. Of the following, the procedure which is MOST essential in maintaining good discipline in the playgrounds is to

    A. establish a definite set of rules
    B. provide interesting games and activities for all groups
    C. punish offenders promptly
    D. establish peer leadership

2.____

3. Of the following, the LEAST important factor to be considered in program planning is

    A. available facilities
    B. total program objectives
    C. skill of participants
    D. availability of volunteer leadership

3.____

4. Of the following, the one that is indispensable for the enjoyment of MOST forms of recreation is

    A. expert performance
    B. seriousness of purpose
    C. a reasonable degree of proficiency
    D. considerable effort

4.____

5. Of the following, the MOST important factor in ensuring safety on trips taken by playground groups is

    A. selecting the safest means of transportation
    B. establishing rules of conduct with the participants before the trip is started
    C. checking on the attendance of the participants frequently during the trip
    D. making sure that the trip is concluded on time

5.____

6. Of the following, a common social characteristic of children in the twelve-to-fourteen-year-old group is that they

    A. often feel misunderstood
    B. accept adult leadership easily
    C. are rarely interested in other people's ideas
    D. seek independence from the peer group

6.____

7. Of the following statements, the one which represents the MOST acceptable statement concerning the relationship of active to passive activities in the playground program is: 7.____

    A. Interest and age groupings should determine the stress that should be given to either active or passive activities
    B. Active and passive activities should each be accorded the same amount of time
    C. Passive activities should be used as a means of providing an interesting rest period
    D. Passive activities should be given emphasis during inclement weather

8. Of the following, the one which represents the BEST statement of policy concerning the inclusion of volleyball in the program of the playground is: 8.____

    A. Volleyball should be a constant activity since every child may participate success-fully
    B. After a period of orientation and motivation, volleyball should be included only if students show an enthusiasm for it
    C. Early exposure, followed by interesting competition, should make volleyball inter-esting to all
    D. The nature of the game is such as to indicate that only the girls are likely to be interested in volleyball over a period of time

9. One group game generates an exceptionally interesting participation on the part of both boys and girls.
Of the following recommendations to the teacher, which is preferred?   9.____

    A. Continue playing the game as long as children are interested.
    B. Rearrange the planned schedule so as to devote unlimited additional time to it.
    C. Continue playing until a majority wants another activity.
    D. Resume the activity after discontinuing it before interest lags.

10. Of the following, a PRIMARY reason for holding a softball tournament among teams of students who attend the playground is that   10.____

    A. competition becomes more meaningful and interesting
    B. tournaments are attractive to spectators
    C. an overall winner can be identified
    D. it keeps many children from getting into trouble

11. Of the following, the MOST significant reason for including tennis instruction in the play-ground program is that it   11.____

    A. provides an excellent all-around exercise
    B. has continuing lifetime value for many individuals
    C. provides many students with a meaningful challenge
    D. is a genteel sport and tends to raise the cultural sights of students

12. Of the following, the MOST effective procedure in bringing children of varying social background into effective social interaction is   12.____

    A. arranging periodic discussions with harmonious interaction as the objective
    B. arranging for the parents of the different groups to meet together
    C. convincing the leadership of these groups that cooperative activity is desirable
    D. arranging for adults to talk to these children

13. Of the following, the MOST important factor in ensuring the success of a tournament conducted in the playground is   13._____

    A. equalizing the potential of teams through a careful selection of team personnel
    B. providing only the most competent officials
    C. involving students intimately in publicity for the tournament
    D. giving teams attractive names

14. Of the following, the LEAST important consideration in organizing groups of children for various physical activities is   14._____

    A. age   B. athletic ability
    C. individual interest   D. size

15. Of the following, the procedure which is MOST likely to ensure the success of a rainy-day program in the playground is   15._____

    A. planning schedules for such a day before the season starts
    B. arranging for moving pictures to consume the time during the rainy period
    C. planning for such a day with a group of children representative of the entire group
    D. consulting with the teacher in charge in ascertaining the nature of programs that have been successful

16. Of the following, the factor which is likely to contribute MOST to making a special events program in the playground a success is to   16._____

    A. provide the teacher in charge of the activity with sufficient time to plan
    B. organize an adequate number of student committees and groups to deal with all aspects of the plan
    C. send written invitations to parents to visit
    D. offer a prize to the student who has contributed most

17. Of the following, the LEAST important factor in the effective selection of physical activities for the playground program is the   17._____

    A. interests of the majority
    B. seasonal factor in various sports
    C. abilities of the group
    D. availability of supplies and facilities

18. Of the following, the LEAST important factor in setting up equipment in a game room is to   18._____

    A. provide for grouping according to the interests of various age levels
    B. consider the safety hazards inherent in the arrangement
    C. facilitate teacher supervision
    D. divide activities according to different interests of boys and girls

19. Of the following, the one which is likely to be MOST successful in assisting children attending the program to grow socially is   19._____

    A. periodic suggestions and admonitions concerning the rights of others
    B. group discussions about the rights of minorities
    C. a program of activities that involves social interplay
    D. a summary at the end of each day stressing the help given one another

20. Of the following, the procedure which is likely to be LEAST important in improving student attendance in the playground is

    A. keeping a roll book and checking attendance morning and afternoon
    B. conferring individually with children who tend to be absent
    C. providing activities based on their appeal to student interests
    D. being pleasant to children at all times

20.____

21. The assistance of adult volunteers in the vacation playground program may be used profitably in all of the following capacities EXCEPT

    A. publicizing center activities
    B. assisting with registration procedures
    C. supervising children on a trip
    D. taking full charge of the physical activities program

21.____

22. Of the following, the BEST procedure for the teacher concerned with developing a meaningful outdoor program of physical activities is to

    A. concentrate on one activity at a time, e.g., the playing of softball
    B. provide a variety of activities in keeping with the limitations of space and facilities
    C. insist that each student participate in each activity on a rotational basis to ensure broad experience
    D. establish definitive plans at the beginning of the season and adhere to them

22.____

23. Of the following, the PRIME purpose of a novelty game is to

    A. afford a sense of success to the non-athletic pupil
    B. appeal to competitive instincts of children
    C. require little space or equipment
    D. provide an easily conducted activity where discipline problems rarely develop

23.____

24. Of the following, the LEAST important purpose of a bulletin board newspaper in the playground is to

    A. make available some of the values of a small group experience
    B. provide recognition and success for some
    C. increase the interest in playground events
    D. develop insight into news reporting as a possible vocation

24.____

25. Of the following, the statement which BEST explains the attitude of thirteen year olds toward coeducational activities is:

    A. Coeducational activities of a social nature appeal but many are shy about participating in them
    B. Girls enjoy such activities, but boys generally do not
    C. Coeducational activities appeal to boys and girls at this age principally in a party atmosphere
    D. Boys and girls are not interested in the same activities at this age

25.____

26. The problem of identifying student leaders for the playground program involves the question of the chronological age group likely to produce effective leaders.
Of the following, which is the statement MOST likely to apply concerning leadership?

26.____

A. Leadership potentials have little relationship to chronological age.
B. The twelve-to-fourteen year old group is ready for opportunities of leadership
C. Leaders should be chosen from among the oldest students in the group
D. Every child has leadership potential

27. In addition to teaching children how to play games provided for the game room area, it is essential that the teacher   27.____

   A. instruct in the proper use of equipment
   B. provide copies of essential rules of the game
   C. organize student leaders to conduct games
   D. suggest how to choose opposing players

28. Of the following, the recommended procedure to follow when playground equipment has been broken is to   28.____

   A. report it at once to the custodian
   B. organize student committees to repair it
   C. remove the equipment
   D. advise students not to use it

29. Of the following, the PRIMARY objective of the playground teacher in introducing a new group game should be to   29.____

   A. develop initially a thorough understanding of the rules so as to minimize conflict
   B. start the group promptly after an understanding of the objectives and the basic rules of the game
   C. develop and practice skills to be used in the game
   D. determine those who are interested so that the others may be given some other activity

30. Of the following, the BEST way to obtain *good discipline* in playground activities as contrasted with *order* is by   30.____

   A. meeting each infraction with prompt and precise action
   B. establishing an understanding of the rationale for regulations
   C. appealing to students through their parents or others
   D. rewarding good conduct in a tangible way

31. Of the following, the BEST way to help a child who displays an undesirable emotional reaction to losing a game is by   31.____

   A. reprimanding him
   B. showing him his error after he has *cooled off*
   C. barring him temporarily from competition
   D. ignoring him completely

32. Of the following, the procedure which is of PRIMARY importance in the conduct of a game room is to   32.____

   A. make sure that no equipment is lost
   B. provide for a system of rotation so that all can participate
   C. avoid the use of too many activities so that supervision is difficult
   D. arrange for boys and girls to participate together

33

33. Of the following, the BEST technique in maintaining attendance in the game room at a high level is to   33._____

    A. announce the schedule well in advance
    B. make the room attractive
    C. organize tournaments in various activities
    D. provide ample bulletin board space

34. Of the following, the BEST procedure to follow in organizing and planning a game room program is to   34._____

    A. consult the teacher-in-charge to determine those activities which have previously proven to be of interest
    B. consider the suggestions made by authorities concerning activities that have been successful
    C. visit other playgrounds to determine the elements of the program that have been successful
    D. involve students in the planning of the program

35. Of the following, the factor which is considered to be the LEAST important in the conduct of a successful game room program is   35._____

    A. a spirit of friendliness
    B. respect for others
    C. an opportunity for self-expression
    D. a spirit of competition

36. Of the following, the MAJOR reason for using pupils in leadership roles in the playground program is to   36._____

    A. assist the teacher in the organization and administration of a broad program
    B. give expression to the leadership potential of students
    C. keep students satisfied with the way matters are handled
    D. keep some students from becoming problems

37. Of the following, the procedure which is of GREATEST importance to the game room teacher planning a series of lessons in table tennis is   37._____

    A. deciding the age level of the children to be included
    B. ascertaining the names of children who are interested
    C. planning the progression of skills to be taught
    D. determining when to start the actual participation of students

38. It is recommended that the game room in a playground be organized so as to   38._____

    A. separate boys and girls
    B. divide students according to the interests of various age levels
    C. allow the teacher to bring groups together readily
    D. provide for easy transfer from one activity to another

39. Of the following, the MOST difficult problem in program planning for the playground is   39._____

    A. providing for small groups within the total program
    B. separating boys' and girls' activities

C. making full use of special facilities
D. encouraging skillful participants to undertake leadership roles

40. Of the following, the MOST serious hazard in a game room area is likely to be   40._____

A. running
C. overcrowding
B. insufficient ventilation
D. age differences

41. Of the following, the LEAST significant value of the games offered in the game room is in   41._____

A. learning to take turns
B. accepting the decision of others
C. widening the circle of friends
D. learning to compete with more able opponents

42. In bowling, the MAXIMUM individual score that it is possible to achieve in one game is   42._____

A. 150   B. 200   C. 250   D. 300

43. All of the following apply to the playing of circle stride ball EXCEPT: 43._____

A. Players stand with feet astride, touching neighbors' feet
B. One player stands in the center of a circle
C. A player may move his feet to block a ball
D. Sometimes the ball is thrown into the circle from outside it

44. All of the following skills are useful in playing the game *Endball* EXCEPT   44._____

A. throwing
C. dribbling
B. catching
D. pivoting

45. In badminton, the server serves   45._____

A. until hand is out
B. until a point is scored
C. until the winning point is scored
D. five times in succession

46. Badminton and tennis are LEAST alike in the   46._____

A. shape of the playing surface
B. use of nets
C. use of rackets
D. method of scoring

47. In regulation play, a match in badminton consists of winning _____ out of _____ games.   47._____

A. two; three
C. three; five
B. three; four
D. four; six

48. A *bird* in badminton falling on a boundary line is considered   48._____

A. *In* court
B. *Out* of court
C. *In* or *Out* dependent on whether the play is a service or volley
D. as requiring a replay if a service

49. Of the following games, the one which requires the LEAST athletic skill is   49._____

   A. volleyball   B. dodgeball
   C. shuffleboard   D. captain ball

50. Of the following scores in tennis, the one which does NOT indicate the completion of a   50._____
   set is

   A. 9-8   B. 6-4   C. 13-11   D. 7-5

51. The type of tournament that provides for competition through challenge is the   51._____

   A. round robin   B. consolation
   C. ladder   D. elimination

52. In order to complete a round robin type tournament with eight teams, the number of   52._____
   games to be played is

   A. 16   B. 24   C. 28   D. 32

53. In volleyball, the manner of rotation of players in position for service is   53._____

   A. front and back   B. counterclockwise
   C. clockwise   D. laterally

54. Safety hazards are implicit in all forms of athletic activities.   54._____
   Of the following, the LEAST important consideration in minimizing these hazards is

   A. a daily inspection of facilities and equipment
   B. the arrangement of activities in the playground
   C. the establishment of regulations concerning costume
   D. a mimeographed list of hazards distributed to participants

55. In volleyball, the *underarm* serve is preferred because it   55._____

   A. is easier to learn
   B. offers a maximum of control
   C. offers as much speed as other serves
   D. is harder to return

56. A player serving in volleyball must comply with all of the following rules EXCEPT: 56._____

   A. Both feet must be behind the back line
   B. The ball must be hit with an open hand
   C. The ball must go clearly over the net
   D. Each member of the team serves in turn

57. In organizing teams for a volleyball tournament in the playground, it is advisable to   57._____
   arrange for a number of players and a few substitutes for each team.
   The basic number, exclusive of substitutes, should be

   A. 6   B. 8   C. 10   D. 12

58. Of the following, the factor which is likely to be MOST productive in making volleyball an   58._____
   interesting and continuing activity among children is

   A. teacher participation
   B. adequate initial motivation

C. individual and group success in playing the game
D. frequent opportunities to play the game

59. In table tennis, when the score is 20-20, a player 59._____

    A. must score two successive points to win
    B. must score the 21st point to win
    C. can score the winning point only while serving
    D. must score 5 additional points to win

60. Of the following, the essential difference between singles and doubles play in table tennis is 60._____

    A. number of points served consecutively by any one player
    B. area to which the serve must be hit
    C. number of points constituting a game
    D. rules governing a *let*

61. In paddle tennis, when both players have won two points, the score is 61._____

    A. three all   B. advantage in or out
    C. thirty all   D. deuce

62. In table tennis, a player loses a point in all of the following situations EXCEPT when he 62._____

    A. fails to make a good service
    B. permits anything on his person to touch the supports for the net while playing the ball
    C. permits his free hand to touch the playing surface while playing the ball
    D. moves from behind the table in returning a ball

63. In a tie game at *20-all* in table tennis, the serve 63._____

    A. continues to be alternated at every five additional points
    B. is alternated on every subsequent point
    C. is alternated after every two additional points
    D. is made by the loser of each subsequent point

64. Of the following, the MOST common error in table tennis is 64._____

    A. failing to be properly poised for the stroke before contact with the ball
    B. standing too close to the table
    C. hitting the ball too softly
    D. confusing the backhand and forehand shots

65. In treating a victim of nosebleed, of the following, the LEAST effective procedure is to 65._____

    A. have the victim lie down immediately
    B. press the nostrils firmly together
    C. apply a large, cold, wet cloth to the nose
    D. pack the nose gently with gauze

66. Sharp cuts that tend to bleed freely are called 66._____

    A. lacerated wounds   B. abrasions
    C. puncture wounds   D. incised wounds

67. The group of symptoms which BEST describes a case of shock is: 67._____

  A. Headache, face flushed, pupils of eyes pinpointed
  B. Pupils of eyes dilated, face cold and moist, pulse weak
  C. Extreme thirst, chills, breathing deep and slow
  D. Reactions irrational, skin dry and warm, pulse slow

68. The score 15-13 could indicate the final score of a completed game in any of the follow- 68._____
ing activities EXCEPT

  A. baseball   B. football
  C. table tennis   D. badminton

69. In performing the back pressure-arm lift method of artificial respiration, the operator 69._____
should _____ of the victim.

  A. kneel at the head   B. straddle both thighs
  C. kneel at either side   D. straddle one thigh

70. The overall purpose of the application of heat to a victim in shock is to 70._____

  A. cause sweating
  B. prevent a large loss of body heat
  C. increase the body's temperature
  D. increase the blood circulation

71. A condition which may result from a deficiency of vitamin C is known as 71._____

  A. beri-beri   B. rickets   C. scurvy   D. impetigo

72. The game in which the winner is determined by the LOWEST score is 72._____

  A. bowling   B. tennis   C. golf   D. badminton

73. In shuffleboard, the discs are shot from the 73._____

  A. base line   B. end line
  C. 10 off are   D. base of the triangle

74. In shuffleboard, all of the following apply EXCEPT 74._____

  A. point values go from seven to ten
  B. discs coming to rest between the starting line and the farthest dead line are
    removed before play is continued
  C. if a singles game ends in a tie, each player then plays two discs from one end
  D. a disc which has come to rest in a scoring area may be driven off

75. In shuffleboard, all of the following apply EXCEPT 75._____

  A. in both singles and doubles, sides alternate in shoving discs
  B. in doubles, partners play at opposite ends of the court
  C. the number of discs used by each side is four in singles and six in doubles
  D. a game consists of fifty points

KEY (CORRECT ANSWERS)

1. A	16. B	31. B	46. D	61. C
2. B	17. B	32. B	47. A	62. D
3. D	18. D	33. C	48. A	63. B
4. C	19. C	34. D	49. C	64. A
5. B	20. A	35. D	50. A	65. A
6. A	21. D	36. B	51. C	66. D
7. B	22. B	37. C	52. C	67. B
8. B	23. A	38. B	53. C	68. C
9. D	24. D	39. A	54. D	69. A
10. A	25. A	40. A	55. B	70. B
11. B	26. B	41. D	56. B	71. C
12. C	27. A	42. D	57. A	72. C
13. A	28. C	43. C	58. C	73. C
14. D	29. B	44. C	59. A	74. C
15. C	30. B	45. A	60. B	75. C

TEST 2

DIRECTIONS: Each question or incomplete statement is followed by several suggested answers or completions. Select the one that BEST answers the question or completes the statement. *PRINT THE LETTER OF THE CORRECT ANSWER IN THE SPACE AT THE RIGHT.*

1. Of the following, the BEST statement of principle concerned with the conduct of the physical activities period in the playground is that   1.____

   A. emphasis should be given to team activities
   B. only intramural as opposed to inter playground competition should be encouraged
   C. each period of physical activities should provide a balance between instructional time and *big muscle activity* time
   D. boys should be given more *big muscle* activities than girls

2. Of the following, the MOST important function of the teacher in the playgrounds is   2.____

   A. officiating at various athletic contests
   B. insuring equality of opportunities of participation
   C. interesting students in a variety of activities
   D. gaining the cooperation of parents

3. Of the following, the LEAST important guiding principle in insuring the success of an athletic competition is to   3.____

   A. equalize as far as possible the athletic potential of each team in the make up of its participants
   B. provide as many opportunities for inter-team competition as possible
   C. provide adequate officiating by having the teacher officiate
   D. provide for effective leadership for each team

4. Of the following, the MOST important factor in insuring safe participation in the activities of the playground is   4.____

   A. a preliminary inspection of the facilities by the teacher each day before the program begins
   B. posting rules and regulations concerned with safety
   C. properly warning students about safety hazards before activities begin
   D. exercising continuing supervision of activities

5. Of the following, the one which is considered to be the MOST important responsibility of the playground teacher is   5.____

   A. planning and conducting activities so as to satisfy the play interests of the majority of children
   B. suggesting new and different activities
   C. insuring the physical growth and development of each child
   D. checking to insure adequate attendance

6. Of the following, the factor MOST apt to result in good discipline in the playground is   6.____

   A. peer leadership
   B. positive teacher direction

    C.   excellent administrative procedure
    D.   an interesting program of activities

7.   Of the following, the LEAST important reason for including a physical activity program in the playgrounds is that it   7.____

    A.   helps develop body organs
    B.   builds muscle tone
    C.   establishes desirable social attitudes
    D.   provides satisfaction in *winning*

8.   Of the following, the MOST effective way to improve the attendance in the playground *game room* is by   8.____

    A.   making it a place for reading and browsing
    B.   allowing only *quiet* games to be played there
    C.   providing a variety of activities, some quiet and others of a semi-active nature
    D.   closing down the *active* areas of the playground periodically

9.   Of the following, the LEAST important reason for a summer playground program is to   9.____

    A.   keep children off the streets
    B.   promote objectives associated with racial integration
    C.   broaden the cultural experiences of children
    D.   provide meaningful recreational experiences

10.   Of the following, the PRIMARY value of motion pictures concerned with sports such as baseball, volleyball, and swimming is to   10.____

    A.   entertain pupils
    B.   develop an interest in the activity
    C.   show students that results are easy to achieve
    D.   assist the teacher to obtain better application

11.   The initial attendance in the vacation playground program is raost satisfactory during the first week, but subsequently falls off alarmingly.   11.____
Of the following, the MOST logical explanation is that the

    A.   teachers have been sympathetic to the problems of the individual
    B.   program does not meet the interests of the participants
    C.   staff has failed to establish enough competitive activities
    D.   participants have found the program too taxing

12.   Of the following considerations, the one which is LEAST important in the selection of activities is   12.____

    A.   alternating active and quiet activities
    B.   placing emphasis on seasonal considerations
    C.   consideration of the mores of the neighborhood served
    D.   preventing any one activity from becoming dominant or too absorbing of interest

13. Of the following, the procedure which is MOST likely to be successful in getting the shy   13._____
    child to participate in activities with others is

    A. a direct confrontation by the teacher in which the advisability of participating is
       pointed out
    B. a patient but persistent encouragement by the teacher
    C. a conference with the parent held with a view to gaining the parent's assistance
    D. having older boys or girls talk to the child

14. Student leaders in the playground may be used for all of the following tasks EXCEPT   14._____

    A. refereeing games
    B. distributing materials
    C. acting as assistants in improving skills performed by other students
    D. opening and closing windows

15. Of the following, the one which is LEAST likely to cause an individual student to become   15._____
    a disciplinary problem in the playground is

    A. lack of success in participation
    B. a sense of insecurity
    C. a poor relationship at home carried over to the playground
    D. a dislike of the activities of interest to other children of the same age

16. When the playground teacher finds that a different child hesitates to compete with others   16._____
    in group games, of the following, the BEST procedure to follow is to

    A. send for a parent to discuss the matter
    B. urge the child to be a good sport and participate
    C. observe the child with a view to determining the cause
    D. report the matter to the teacher-in-charge

17. Of the following, the method considered to be LEAST effective in the teaching of motor   17._____
    skills is

    A. analysis on the part of the teacher
    B. demonstration by a participant
    C. imitation
    D. a verbal description of the skill

18. Of the following, the MAJOR advantage in the use of games of low organization is that   18._____

    A. relatively unskilled players may gain satisfaction in competing
    B. the teacher may supervise these more efficiently than other activities
    C. safety hazards are reduced
    D. large playground areas may be used more efficiently

19. Of the following elements of successful play experience, the one which is the SLOWEST   19._____
    to develop among young children is

    A. interest in participation
    B. a spirit of competition
    C. a sense of cooperative enterprise
    D. absence of undue concern about physical well-being

20. Rainy day programs in the playground should

    A. be limited to quiet games
    B. make effective use of indoor space for both active and quiet games
    C. be such as to limit attendance
    D. consist of assembly programs and the use of motion pictures

20._____

21. Of the following, concerning spectator participation in the activities of the playground, the one which represents the MOST acceptable position is that spectators should be

    A. discouraged
    B. urged to become participants
    C. unnoticed
    D. invited to view special competitions

21._____

22. Of the following, the manner in which parental assistance can be MOST effectively utilized is by

    A. officiating at activities of various kinds
    B. accompanying a group to a museum
    C. preparing a playground newspaper
    D. coaching a dramatics performance

22._____

23. Of the following statements concerning athletic activities to be included in the program of the playground, the one which is the LEAST valid is:

    A. Activities should have *carry-over* values
    B. Only those activities that are devoid of all safety hazards should be included
    C. Activities included can be identified with the interests of chronological age groups
    D. Activities should be related to differing interests based on sex

23._____

24. Of the following, concerning the use of the teacher's whistle, the one which represents the BEST advice is that

    A. the whistle should be used infrequently. When used, it should be blown with incisiveness
    B. a whistle can be used effectively to stop activities and simultaneously to provide *directions*
    C. a whistle should never be blown harshly
    D. the tone and incisiveness of whistle blowing should be varied

24._____

25. Of the following, the factor that is MOST apt to reflect the degree of interest shown by a group of children in a particular game is the

    A. motivation supplied by the teachers
    B. degree of success achieved
    C. length of time of participation
    D. degree of activity provided

25._____

26. Of the following, the PRIMARY value of a well-organized program in the playgrounds is that

    A. disciplinary problems are minimized
    B. it helps to insure a maximum of values for the participants

26._____

    C.   the time of the participants is fully taken up
    D.   good attendance is insured

27. A participant under your jurisdiction in the playground abuses equipment several times.   27._____
A typical example of this is *kicking a basketball.*
Of the following, the BEST way to handle the situation after his failure to heed your initial warning is to

    A.   send for his parents
    B.   bar him from further participation
    C.   question him privately in an effort to get him to understand that his actions are wrong
    D.   report him to the teacher in charge for disciplinary action

28. A teacher assigned to cooperate with you in developing and supervising your program   28._____
frequently *disappears* and fails to accept his responsibilities.
Of the following, the BEST way to handle the situation is to

    A.   warn him at the earliest opportunity to make certain that this behavior ceases
    B.   report him to your *immediate superior* with the request that he *speak* to your colleague
    C.   point out the difficulties that his absence creates for you and your students
    D.   do the best you can without him and wait for your superior to note his failure to carry out his duties

29. *Assemblies* in the playground schedule of activities are MOST important in that they   29._____

    A.   provide periods of *quiet* activity
    B.   develop a community spirit
    C.   give children important information
    D.   promote individual interests

30. Of the following, the MOST important result of a well-planned vital program in the play-   30._____
ground is that it

    A.   contributes to the cultural education of the participants
    B.   promotes good attendance
    C.   continues the work of the regular school
    D.   provides a safe place for children to spend the day

31. Of the following procedures, the one which is considered LEAST valuable in the conduct   31._____
of the daily playground program is

    A.   calling children together to present and share their experiences of the day
    B.   holding *assemblies* to present dramatic programs
    C.   keeping an accurate attendance record for each individual child
    D.   conducting a preliminary *safety check*

32. Of the following, the LEAST important reason for grouping children on a chronological   32._____
basis is that

    A.   interests vary
    B.   safe participation can be promoted

C. teaching techniques vary with age levels
D. the teachers' organizational problems are made easier

33. Of the following, the LEAST important principle in conducting a program of movies for showing in the playground program is that 33.____

    A. movies should be scheduled for a regular time each week
    B. the movies selected should be entertaining as well as educational
    C. movies should be previewed by the teacher
    D. some of the pictures selected for viewing should be related to the other activities of the playground

34. Of the following, the LEAST important consideration in planning the athletic program of the playground is 34.____

    A. the facilities that are available
    B. the age groups of the participants
    C. seasonal interests
    D. the skill and ability of the teacher in the activities selected

35. Of the following responsibilities of the playground teacher, the one which is FIRST in importance is to 35.____

    A. provide activities for the participation of the maximum number
    B. emphasize big muscle activity
    C. give individual instruction
    D. introduce new activities

36. The playground teacher who is about to introduce a new game will generally find that the BEST way to arouse interest is to 36.____

    A. explain the history of the game
    B. outline the object of the game
    C. tell why he enjoyed the game
    D. tell the children that it is a game they will enjoy

37. Of the following, the factor which should exert the LEAST influence on the length of the play period in the playground is 37.____

    A. the age of the participants
    B. the degree of interest demonstrated
    C. the number of children and the facilities available
    D. whether it is conducted during the morning or afternoon sessions

38. Of the following, a PRIME objective of the teacher in the vacation playground should be to 38.____

    A. develop sound social attributes
    B. teach the rules of group games
    C. entertain children
    D. prevent discord

39. Of the following, the MOST important objective of a trip to a fair by a group of children under your supervision is the

    A. broadening of educational and cultural backgrounds
    B. relieving of the monotony of a daily playground schedule
    C. rewarding of good behavior
    D. learning of how to behave as a member of a group

40. Your playground serves children from two segregated areas. You find that the children tend to remain segregated in the playground.
    Of the following, the BEST way to meet this issue is to

    A. point out to them the importance of effective integration
    B. provide assembly programs with integration as the theme
    C. consult with the parents of the respective groups
    D. provide activities that develop a common sphere of interest

41. Of the following, the MOST effective way to develop good sportsmanship in the playground is by

    A. praising evidences of good sportsmanship as these develop
    B. outlining to a group the qualities to be encouraged
    C. showing how good sportsmanship is always rewarded
    D. emphasizing the relative importance of winning as compared to sportsmanship

42. Of the following principles concerning the conduct of the playground program, the one which is of PRIMARY importance is that the

    A. teacher should pre-plan activities
    B. individual participant should be afforded an opportunity to choose activities
    C. activities chosen should be seasonal in nature
    D. outdoor facilities should be used in good weather

43. Of the following, the generally accepted reason for insisting that children be properly instructed in their initial experiences in such activities as golf and tennis is to

    A. prevent them from establishing incorrect habits
    B. provide participation on a safe basis
    C. provide for gradual development in the execution of the skills involved
    D. promote effective interests in the activity

44. The round robin tournament should be used instead of the elimination tournament

    A. when time is not a factor and the number of teams is small
    B. to provide opportunities for better sportsmanlike participation
    C. when younger participants are involved
    D. when participants want to develop greater skill

45. Of the following, the PRIME importance of tournament programs in team activities is that they

    A. provide a schedule for improving skills of individual participants
    B. develop social skills

C. stimulate interest in active participation
D. determine a winner

46. The *ladder* type of tournament is especially useful in conducting competition in   46.____

    A. table tennis   B. softball
    C. basketball   D. football

47. Of the following games, the one which requires equipment other than a ball is   47.____

    A. dodge ball   B. overhead relay
    C. call ball   D. bombardment

48. All of the following are associated with playing the game of CIRCLE STRIDE BALL   48.____
EXCEPT

    A. having adjacent players touch feet
    B. keeping the hands on the knees during part of the play
    C. having someone who is *It*
    D. keeping the body in a semi-crouched position

49. UNDER-LEGS RELAY, OVERHEAD RELAY, and ZIG-ZAG RELAY are activities of low   49.____
organization that emphasize particularly skill in

    A. throwing   B. passing
    C. dribbling   D. shooting

50. The game AROUND THE WORLD is MOST closely associated with   50.____

    A. HARE AND HOUNDS   B. FARMER IN THE DELL
    C. basketball   D. SPUD

51. Of the following team or group activities, the one of GREATEST competitive interest for   51.____
ten-year-old boys is

    A. volleyball   B. table tennis
    C. softball   D. snatch the club

52. In the game of dodgeball, of the following, the factor of LEAST importance in insuring   52.____
safe participation is the

    A. size of the circle
    B. number of participants
    C. degree of inflation of the ball used
    D. speed of the participants

53. Of the following, the activity which provides a child with the BEST opportunity to practice   53.____
skills in which he has not reached a degree of proficiency is

    A. the *free enterprise* period
    B. the playing of a game
    C. a squad activities period
    D. an activity in which the individual is assigned leadership roles

54. Which of the following statements is true about the group game known as THREE DEEP?
It is a game

    A. played in a circle formation
    B. that uses *spare* players
    C. employing a *hide and seek* technique
    D. in which the third player throws a ball

54._____

55. Of the following games, the one which employs the LARGEST ball is

    A. volleyball   B. pushball
    C. basketball   D. dodgeball

55._____

56. The game END BALL requires

    A. guards and basemen
    B. several basketballs
    C. a large basketball court
    D. at least two referees

56._____

57. Of the following, the MOST important reason for introducing *lead-up* games is that they

    A. engage larger numbers
    B. provide greater satisfaction
    C. tend to sustain greater interest
    D. provide practice in essential skills

57._____

58. Of the following games, the one which employs the FEWEST and SIMPLEST rules is

    A. End Ball   B. handball
    C. Spud   D. volleyball

58._____

59. The term *lob* is used in all of the following sports EXCEPT

    A. handball   B. tennis
    C. badminton   D. volleyball

59._____

60. A game in which competitors are required to keep *feet touching those of adjacent players* is

    A. Circle Stride Ball   B. dodgeball
    C. Newcomb   D. Spud

60._____

61. KEEP-AWAY is a group game that provides practice in

    A. passing a ball   B. tagging opponents
    C. striking a target   D. kicking a ball

61._____

62. SPUD is a game that includes all of the following EXCEPT

    A. the numbering of players   B. throwing a ball
    C. running   D. selecting partners

62._____

63. Of the following relay races, the type which requires a tandem arrangement of competitors is

    A. Wheelbarrow   B. All Up Relay
    C. Circle Relay   D. Pass Ball Relay

63._____

64. In badminton, points are scored

    A. by either the serving or receiving side
    B. only by the serving side
    C. not until two serves have been made
    D. in a fashion similar to table tennis

64._____

65. All of the following are true in the playing of newcomb EXCEPT:

    A. Teams of 8 to 14 players may be used to advantage
    B. A rope may be used instead of a net
    C. The ball may be relayed between players on the same side
    D. The ball may not touch the net or rope

65._____

66. Of the following, the LEAST important reason for including paddle tennis in a playground program is that

    A. it requires relatively little space
    B. the equipment used is inexpensive and durable
    C. it provides a good background experience for lawn tennis
    D. it is a vigorous activity

66._____

67. In badminton, all of the following apply EXCEPT:

    A. The server may stand outside of his court
    B. The serve must be made with an underhand stroke
    C. If the server makes a fault, he is out
    D. A game may consist of fifteen or twenty-one points

67._____

68. In volleyball, a serve is good if it

    A. is hit by any part of the hand or fist from behind the end line over the net and into the opponent's court
    B. touches the net after being hit by an open hand
    C. is hit by one or both hands over the net and into the opponent's court
    D. is hit over the net from any one of the six player's position, using an open hand

68._____

69. All of the following statements are true of the serve in badminton EXCEPT:

    A. Either an underhand or an overhead swing of the racket is permitted
    B. The server continues to serve until he makes a fault or his opponent scores an *ace*
    C. A successful serve must fall between a *short* and a *long* service line
    D. A shuttle may not be hit twice in succession by the server

69._____

70. Of the following, which pair of games is MOST similar in method of play?

    A. Deck tennis - Newcomb   B. Basketball - soccer
    C. Volleyball - tennis   D. Paddle tennis - handball

70._____

49

71. The American Red Cross recommends that an abrasion be treated by

    A. applying iodine
    B. covering the wound with gauze
    C. washing the wound with soap and water
    D. applying mercurochrome

71._____

72. Of the following, the contagious disease of the skin that the playground teacher should recognize in order to protect others is

    A. conjunctivitis
    B. lordosis
    C. Osgood Schlatter's disease
    D. impetigo

72._____

73. Of the following, the symptom of heatstroke MOST frequently noted is

    A. an absence of perspiration
    B. mental confusion
    C. headache
    D. dilated pupils

73._____

74. A puncture wound is considered serious from the point of view that

    A. bleeding may be hard to stop
    B. injury to tissue may be extensive
    C. infection is likely to result
    D. multiple injury may result

74._____

75. The method of resuscitation MOST generally accepted today is the _____ method.

    A. back pressure-arm lift   B. mouth to mouth
    C. Silvester   D. Schaefer

75._____

KEY (CORRECT ANSWERS)

1.	C	16.	C	31.	C	46.	A	61.	A
2.	C	17.	D	32.	D	47.	D	62.	D
3.	C	18.	A	33.	A	48.	D	63.	A
4.	D	19.	C	34.	D	49.	C	64.	B
5.	A	20.	B	35.	A	50.	C	65.	C
6.	D	21.	D	36.	B	51.	C	66.	C
7.	D	22.	B	37.	D	52.	D	67.	A
8.	C	23.	B	38.	A	53.	A	68.	A
9.	A	24.	A	39.	A	54.	A	69.	A
10.	B	25.	B	40.	D	55.	B	70.	A
11.	B	26.	B	41.	A	56.	A	71.	C
12.	D	27.	C	42.	B	57.	D	72.	D
13.	B	28.	C	43.	A	58.	C	73.	A
14.	D	29.	B	44.	A	59.	D	74.	C
15.	D	30.	B	45.	C	60.	A	75.	B

EXAMINATION SECTION
TEST 1

DIRECTIONS: Each question or incomplete statement is followed by several suggested answers or completions. Select the one that BEST answers the question or completes the statement. *PRINT THE LETTER OF THE CORRECT ANSWER IN THE SPACE AT THE RIGHT.*

1. A *typical* definition of recreation agreed upon by MOST authorities would be   1.____

   A. voluntarily chosen leisure activities, for pleasure or personal benefit, meeting community standards and needs
   B. pleasurable activities provided by community agencies without social purpose
   C. whatever people want to do, because they want to do it
   D. purposeful activities, such as anti-delinquency, addiction treatment or golden age programs, which make use of trips and cultural activities

2. In the past, it was argued that recreation programs for youth prevented juvenile delinquency.   2.____
   Today the majority of social work or recreation authorities would MOST probably support the view that

   A. recreation is the key element in any anti-delinquency program
   B. recreation has proved to be of little value in anti-delinquency programs
   C. juvenile delinquents usually are anti-social and disruptive and should be kept out of organized recreation programs
   D. juvenile delinquency treatment requires varied services, including education, job training, recreation, and improved housing

3. The MAJOR professional organization serving the recreation field in the United States today is the   3.____

   A. American Institute of Park and Recreation Practitioners
   B. National Recreation and Park Association
   C. National Recreation Association
   D. American Association for Health, Physical Education, and Recreation

4. Varied theories of play have been developed by psychologists, philosophers, and others.   4.____
   One TRADITIONAL theory that sees play as the means through which children prepare for the demands of adult life is the _____ theory.

   A. instinct-practice   B. catharsis
   C. recapitulation   D. relaxation

5. Which of the following statements BEST supports the self-expression theory of play as developed by Mason and Mitchell?   5.____

   A. Activities are engaged in for the purpose of overcoming natural human inertness.
   B. Due to the pressures for self-maintenance and other compulsions, human beings use play as outlets for frustration.
   C. Human physiological and anatomical structure are independent of any specific form of play.
   D. Because human beings are dynamic animals, activity is a primary need of life.

6. Of the following, the MOST recent psychological theory of play is the   6._____

    A. pleasure principle theory (Freud)
    B. play extraversion theory (Piaget)
    C. arousal or stimulation theory (Berlynne)
    D. aggressive-release theory (Schiller-Spencer-Groos)

7. Generally, the BASIC philosophy of public recreation departments today is to   7._____

    A. serve all groups as fully as possible
    B. place the greatest emphasis on helping the poor
    C. serve primarily the middle and upper classes
    D. concentrate on children and youth

8. The one of the following which is NOT a widely accepted goal of public recreation depart-   8._____
   ments is to

    A. provide constructive and creative outlets for leisure
    B. meet participants' physical, mental, social, and creative needs
    C. develop large numbers of athletes to play on college or pro teams
    D. strengthen family life and help build community unity

9. The growth of the organized recreation movement in the United States was promoted by   9._____
   several social factors.
   Of the following, the one which did NOT contribute to such growth is

    A. the increase in leisure through the shortened work-week, more holidays, and
       longer vacations
    B. the development of movies, television, and radio as major forms of entertainment
    C. the general affluence and mobility in society
    D. more liberal attitudes toward leisure on the part of religious, educational, and gov-
       ernment authorities

10. Recognition by state certifying boards or departments is one of the formal methods   10._____
    through which professionals in fields such as law or medicine are approved.
    Today, certification for recreation professionals exists in

    A. a small number of states   B. all fifty states
    C. no states   D. about half the states

11. Supervisors should be able to advise recently appointed recreation workers on the   11._____
    appropriate selection of activities for specific age groups.
    When planning for after-school recreation activities for boys of elementary-school age,
    the MOST useful type of game would usually be

    A. low-organized games, such as dodge-ball, kick-ball, and relays
    B. table games, such as parcheesi, backgammon, and chess
    C. encounter games and touching games, like those used in sensitivity groups
    D. mental games and contests, such as ghost, coffee-pot, and twenty questions

12. Since anti-social youth are often unwilling to enter highly structured activities and pro-   12._____
    grams, or may be barred from recreation centers, they are frequently not served by com-
    munity recreation agencies.
    Of the following, the BEST way to serve such youth is to

    A.   develop entirely new kinds of activities that will appeal to delinquents because of their thrill-seeking nature

    B.   organize special community center programs to serve only delinquent youth who have been in trouble with the law

    C.   assign roving or street gang workers to make contact with unaffiliated youth and gangs to involve them in constructive activities

    D.   wait until they are sent to correctional institutions and then give them concentrated recreation programs there

13.   Adolescent girls in youth houses (detention or remand centers) often have poor self-concepts.   13.____
Of the following, the TYPICAL approach used by recreation workers in such settings to help these girls improve their self-concepts is to

    A.   tell such girls at appropriate times that they are just as good as anybody

    B.   organize self-improvement classes to teach skills in make-up, dressing, or modeling

    C.   sponsor sports teams, such as basketball or volleyball, which can compete with other institutions

    D.   administer personality tests to diagnose their problems

14.   Many teen-age boys are fascinated by automobiles.   14.____
Of the following, a USEFUL way for a recreation worker to deal with this interest would be to

    A.   sponsor drag-racing meets in a conveniently located park or raceway

    B.   develop an automotive hobby car repair club in a community center or nearby garage

    C.   arrange a contest to select one boy to go on a trip to the Indianapolis 500 to watch the big race

    D.   develop a joint program with a school bus company to train boys as junior bus operators

15.   According to the traditional *space standards* employed for the past several decades to   15.____
measure the need for open space and recreation facilities in American communities, there should be AT LEAST

    A.   one neighborhood playground for each 1,500 children under age 12

    B.   three acres of outdoor recreation space for each 1,000 residents

    C.   one acre of outdoor recreation space for each 100 residents

    D.   one community center for each 5,000 children and teen-agers

16.   *Therapeutic recreation service* is the term applied today to programs which serve the   16.____
physically, mentally, or socially handicapped.
For BEST results, such programs should be provided in

    A.   institutions such as mental hospitals or schools for the retarded

    B.   community settings such as after-care centers or community programs for the physically disabled

    C.   both institutional and community settings

    D.   private or voluntary facilities

17. Social group work is BEST defined as a method of social work which   17.____

    A. assigns people to groups for intensive psychotherapy as a means of crisis intervention

    B. helps people improve their social functioning and ability to cope with inter-personal problems

    C. utilizes unskilled community people to take over many social work organizations

    D. relies on the leader's ability to mobilize people into effective instruments for community reform

18. Some recreation departments operate multi-service senior centers which provide social   18.____
services related to nutrition, health needs, legal, or housing assistance, as well as recreation.
This type of program is regarded by leading authorities in the field of recreation as

    A. usually not the function of a recreation department since it has proved to be a hindrance to customary social and recreational programs

    B. clearly not the function of a recreation department and should be discontinued

    C. an appropriate function of a recreation department and is justified by Federal funding guidelines in this field

    D. an appropriate function of a recreation department only when the program is receiving a grant from the State Department of Aging

19. The view that MOST social workers *generally* have of recreation is that it is   19.____

    A. almost identical to social work

    B. a competitor with social work for public funds

    C. a medium through which they can involve and work constructively with participants

    D. strictly for fun, without a serious purpose

20. The three MAJOR areas of social work training and practice are   20.____

    A. group work, psychiatric case work, and neighborhood management

    B. community analysis, case work, and agency supervision

    C. group rehabilitation, psychiatric community development, and case work

    D. case work, group work, and community organization

21. Which of the following BEST expresses the program objectives of recreation programs   21.____
provided by the municipal agencies as a whole?
They should

    A. emphasize after-school and summer vacation play programs

    B. provide activities for various age groups

    C. concentrate on programs for younger boys and teenage youth

    D. meet social needs that are unsatisfied by family relationships

22. Of the following, which is the LEAST appropriate basis for choosing the recreation program activities for a community center, hospital, or other institutions?   22.____
The

    A. needs and interests of the participants based on their age, sex, socio-economic background, etc.

    B. overall philosophy and goals of the sponsoring agency

C. ability of the agency to offer certain activities based on its staff resources, facilities, funding, etc.

D. degree to which prospective participants are personally acquainted with one another

23. The MOST common approach to developing schedules of program activities in municipal recreation departments is to organize them

    23.____

    A. on a centralized basis, that is, each central office or county headquarters develops a precise schedule that must be followed in each center or playground

    B. on a *report* system, that is, each center or playground develops its individual schedule and must report daily on which activities were carried out and which were not

    C. on the basis of seasonal interests, with different schedules being developed for summer, fall, winter, and spring

    D. according to whatever seems to be of interest on a particular day, emphasizing flexibility

24. A difficult problem in scheduling recreation programs is to have personnel available at needed times.
The BEST approach for dealing with this problem is to

    24.____

    A. change recreation leadership jobs to the four-day workweek that has become so popular in industry

    B. make leadership assignment schedules more flexible to insure coverage for special events, including evening and weekend activities

    C. assign all personnel a noon-to-8 P.M. daily schedule

    D. convert all full-time leadership jobs into part-time per session positions and then assign these as needed

25. Ideally, the BEST program schedule for a community recreation center would be one which covers

    25.____

    A. the full day and evening to permit scheduling for senior citizens, housewives, or pre-schoolers, as well as youth and other adults

    B. from 3:00 P.M. to 10:00 P.M. since this is the time when children and youth are out of school

    C. the daily hours of maximum use, based on participant demand, because of the financial limitations of many centers

    D. daytime hours only since most people today will not come out at night because of fear of crime

———

KEY (CORRECT ANSWERS)

1.	A	11.	A
2.	D	12.	C
3.	B	13.	B
4.	A	14.	B
5.	D	15.	C
6.	C	16.	C
7.	A	17.	B
8.	C	18.	C
9.	B	19.	C
10.	A	20.	D

21.	B
22.	D
23.	C
24.	B
25.	A

TEST 2

DIRECTIONS: Each question or incomplete statement is followed by several suggested answers or completions. Select the one that BEST answers the question or completes the statement. *PRINT THE LETTER OF THE CORRECT ANSWER IN THE SPACE AT THE RIGHT.*

1. Active team games during the summer months of July and August at a neighborhood playground are BEST scheduled for   1.____

    A. early afternoon and late evening
    B. Saturday only (morning and afternoon)
    C. morning, late afternoon, and evening
    D. evening only (after 7:30 P.M.)

2. Various activities help to keep attendance at a summer playground high by building interest and enthusiasm among participants.   2.____
Which of the following is the POOREST example of such activities?

    A. Weekly special events, such as pet shows, bicycle rodeos, hobby fairs, etc.
    B. End-of-summer festivals, carnivals, play-days, exhibitions, etc., for which participants prepare for several weeks
    C. Trips using chartered or public transportation to state parks, swimming pools, etc. for those attending regularly
    D. Daily tutoring programs of remedial education for those who are having difficulty in school

3. Of the various types of activities sponsored by public recreation departments, the MOST popular single category, according to national surveys, is   3.____

    A. services for the handicapped (such as the mentally retarded, blind, or physically disabled)
    B. the performing arts (music, drama, and dance)
    C. social activities (clubs, parties, dances, etc.)
    D. sports of all kinds (such as baseball, football, and basketball)

4. The MOST typical method of organizing youth sports leagues in public recreation departments is to   4.____

    A. encourage recreation leaders to organize and coach several teams themselves, running their own tournaments
    B. reduce competitive play, which is harmful to youth, and concentrate instead on cooperative games
    C. work with community organizations that set up and coach their own teams
    D. have children on each block form their own teams and do their own coaching

5. Each craft activity has a specific set of terms describing its equipment or process.   5.____
The following words, *bisque, greenware,* and *slab-construction,* are used in reference to

    A. ceramics   B. metalcrafts
    C. glass-blowing   D. decoupage

6. According to their degree of difficulty, various arts and crafts activities are usually suited   6.___
   to different age levels. Which of the following would be MOST suited to pre-school children?

   A. Macrame   B. Water-color painting
   C. Fingerpainting   D. Jewelry-making

7. Among the most popular recreational sport activities are basketball, baseball, and bowl-   7.___
   ing.
   The terms which do NOT apply to any of these three games are

   A. strike, dribble, sacrifice
   B. linebacker, offside, foot-fault
   C. spare, infield, hoop
   D. walking, infield, alley

8. Which of the following activities would LEAST likely be found in a municipal recreation   8.___
   department's music program?

   A. Rock-and-roll band practice and competition
   B. Chamber music groups
   C. Drum and bugle corps
   D. Informal community singing or folk music activities

9. Informal dramatics activities are often used with children and teenagers.   9.___
   Which of the following would be MOST likely to promote creative dramatic skills and
   interest among beginners?

   A. One-act play contests with scripts, costumes, and scenery
   B. Choral reading of popular poetry
   C. Memorizing and reciting sections from famous Broadway plays
   D. Improvisational dramatic games, like prop or paper bag plays

10. In the past, many recreation departments sponsored holiday festivals or special events   10.___
    such as the English May Day Festival.
    Today, the trend is to

    A. have such festivals reflect ethnic group interests such as Black Culture or His-
        panic-American Arts
    B. eliminate all such events since there is little interest in them
    C. deal mainly with historical commemorations since these would appeal to traditional
        patriotism
    D. make festivals *future-minded* by dealing with the Space Age or America of the
        Future

11. Of the following types of tournaments, the type which can be completed MOST quickly in   11.___
    individual sports such as fencing or table-tennis is the _____ tournament.

    A. round robin   B. elimination
    C. challenge (pyramid)   D. challenge (ladder)

12. Recreation has been affected by several key trends in psychiatric treatment.   12.____
Which of the following is NOT such a key trend?

    A. Reducing patient populations in large, distant state institutions and setting up local mental health facilities, with after-care or day-clinic programs
    B. Reliance on chemotherapy, which makes patients more receptive to programs
    C. The development of activity therapy programs in many hospitals, which include education, recreation, occupational therapy, and similar activities
    D. Hiring of psychiatric patients as recreation aides, which may lead to employment after discharge

13. In recreation programs serving the seriously physically handicapped, such as those who   13.____
have suffered strokes, amputations, etc., the PRIMARY program objective is to

    A. help patients develop potential skills using the facilities of community and out-of-hospital recreational programs
    B. raise funds, through parties, bazaars, special shows, etc., that patients put on to meet special patient needs
    C. use recreation as a specific treatment modality that will restore function, help patients learn to use prosthesis, etc.
    D. make patients accept their limitations and the fact that they cannot participate in many normal recreation activities

14. The majority of retarded teen-agers or young adults live in the community, rather than in   14.____
institutions. Recreation for such persons has several important goals.
Of the following, the LEAST appropriate recreation goal for such retardates is to

    A. help them improve the poor coordination and overcome the obesity typical of many retardates through physical activity
    B. help them acquire social skills and improve behavior and appearance so they will be able to mingle with others more effectively
    C. provide enjoyable and socially desirable leisure activities in order to make life more satisfying
    D. improve their I.Q.'s in order to help them get better jobs or be able to continue in school

15. Senior centers that serve older persons should meet the important needs of these indi-   15.____
viduals.
Of the following, it would be LEAST appropriate for such centers to meet the need for

    A. full-time employment by acting as a placement bureau for center members
    B. modified physical activity to help keep older people active and prevent physical deterioration
    C. social activity to help aging people make friends and avoid isolation
    D. program activities in which older people may do volunteer service in hospitals or in the community

16. In planning a recreation program at a low-income public housing project, it is important to   16.____
establish an advisory board or council.
Such board or council should represent PRIMARILY the needs and interests of the local

    A. civic groups   B. residents
    C. parent-teacher associations   D. youth workers

17. Public relations may have many objectives for a public recreation department. Of the following, the LEAST appropriate objective would be to

    A. provide accurate information about the department's overall program to the public at large

    B. encourage attendance and involvement at the department's events and regular programs

    C. build favorable public attitudes and encourage volunteer leadership in the programs

    D. encourage petitions or letter-writing campaigns for increased budgets for the department

17.___

18. The one of the following which is the MOST effective method for producing successful public relations is for recreation program administrators to

    A. appear before civic organizations

    B. satisfy users of programs

    C. publish effective brochures, announcements, and reports

    D. employ qualified, indigenous para-professionals

18.___

19. If a recreation supervisor were going to publicize a large one-day recreation event in his borough, the BEST way to promote attendance would be to

    A. use newspaper releases and distribute fliers to schools, churches, and temples

    B. place posters advertising the event in store windows

    C. put posters on playground bulletin boards

    D. make a filmstrip about the forthcoming event and distribute prints to civic groups

19.___

20. Assume that, as a recreation supervisor, you are directing a community center that has poor participation in programs by local residents.
Of the following, the MOST effective way for you to arouse more public interest would be to

    A. have the publicity office in your department's central office send out newspaper releases about the center

    B. form a neighborhood council to interpret the community's needs to you and help publicize your program

    C. frequent places where local people congregate

    D. plan a panel discussion in a nearby community auditorium to discuss the problem

20.___

21. There are several possible approaches to getting community involvement in recreation service.
Of the following, the approach that would usually be LEAST workable would be to

    A. draw up a list of interested parents, clergymen, businessmen, local educators, etc., and invite them to a planning meeting about the neighborhood's recreation program

21.___

B.   announce an election to a recreation council, and select a slate of nominees, one for each square block so that local residents can elect their own representatives
C.   inquire as to whether the local Parent-Teachers Association will form a subcommittee interested in youth recreation to assist you
D.   work closely with the local district planning board to insure that they consider recreation as an important community service and to get their advice and help

22. Whether patients will be able to use their leisure constructively after discharge from the hospital is of vital concern to recreation workers in psychiatric hospitals.
Which of the following approaches would be LEAST useful in assuring continuing recreation service to a patient?   22._____

A.   Get a mimeographed list of recreation agencies in a patient's neighborhood and give him this before he is discharged.
B.   Visit and talk with staff members of recreation agencies in a patient's neighborhood to make plans for their receiving the discharged patient.
C.   Develop joint hospital-community recreation programs in special events, tours, entertainment programs, etc. to build a base of understanding for discharged patients
D.   Help the patient develop skills and interests in activities that will actually be available in his neighborhood after discharge

23. Therapeutic recreation seeks to help disabled persons enjoy a fuller, happier life. The question of whether they should be segregated in separate programs for the handicapped is an important one.
Which of the following statements about this group is MOST valid?   23._____

A.   The non-handicapped in society are usually very sympathetic to the disabled and welcome them in all recreational and social programs
B.   The handicapped are better off by themselves, in groups with others having similar disabilities, so they will not feel inferior.
C.   It is an important goal to integrate the handicapped with other persons whenever possible, although sometimes it may not be feasible.
D.   The handicapped should, without exception, be mixed with the non-handicapped in recreation programs.

24. Recreation is usually considered to be a positive force for improving social relations between different racial, ethnic, or socio-economic groups.
Of the following, which is the MOST valid statement about recreation and inter-group relations?   24._____

A.   Public recreation is one field in which racial discrimination is not prohibited by law.
B.   Recreation workers have an obligation to reflect and agree with the views of those they serve, regardless of the nature of such views.
C.   Many of our community recreation programs are heavily racially segregated.
D.   Prejudice is an inborn trait which often appears in competitive sports.

25. For minority-group youth, sports often provide upward social mobility into college and subsequent business careers.
    However, of the following, a MAJOR problem that arises for such youth in their seeking upward social mobility is that

    A. unscrupulous college sports programs often exploit them
    B. they are unable to satisfactorily relate to members of their peer group
    C. sports fail to provide an outlet for hostility and aggression
    D. religious cults to which they become converted distract them from sports

25.____

_____

KEY (CORRECT ANSWERS)

1.	C	11.	B
2.	D	12.	D
3.	D	13.	A
4.	C	14.	D
5.	A	15.	A
6.	C	16.	B
7.	B	17.	D
8.	B	18.	B
9.	D	19.	A
10.	A	20.	B

21.	B
22.	A
23.	C
24.	C
25.	A

_____

TEST 3

DIRECTIONS: Each question or incomplete statement is followed by several suggested answers or completions. Select the one that BEST answers the question or completes the statement. *PRINT THE LETTER OF THE CORRECT ANSWER IN THE SPACE AT THE RIGHT.*

1. The trend in many recreation and park departments during the past several years has been toward providing special facilities and programs based on user fees and charges. The criticism MOST often made against such fees and charges is that

    A. few recreation directors have made serious efforts to serve residents of disadvantaged neighborhoods
    B. it increases the cost of servicing and maintaining facilities and services because standards must be raised
    C. public employees may be tempted to misappropriate funds or may be subject to accusations of dishonesty
    D. poor people may be unable to participate in what should be a publicly-available service

1.____

2. With few exceptions, recreation directors have not been able to gain permission to operate programs regularly in school buildings.
Of the following, the MOST successful way to improve this situation is to

    A. develop relationships and cooperative programs with the local school board and district officials, or with individual school principals and custodians
    B. bring a class action suit against the local school board
    C. collect and submit legally valid petitions to the administration
    D. exert pressure on the schools by denying them use of parks or other recreational facilities for their physical education activities

2.____

3. Many hospitals, particularly psychiatric hospitals, have therapists keep regular reports of patient participation in recreation programs.
Of the following, the BEST use of such reports is to

    A. provide information which may be presented at meetings of the treatment team when the progress of patients is discussed
    B. provide a basis for a daily discussion between the patient and the therapist so the patient knows what is expected of him
    C. justify adverse actions such as denial of recreation privileges or the imposition of personal restrictions
    D. meet the requirements of mental hygiene laws as to standards of treatment and patient progress

3.____

4. Much correspondence is likely to come into the central office of a public recreation department.
Generally, all letters should be answered within one or two days UNLESS

    A. a letter is of a commonplace and unimportant nature
    B. the writer is unreasonably critical of the department
    C. form letters are used in place of personalized correspondence
    D. a letter requires special inquiries or decision-making

4.____

5. One major type of report in recreation programs is based on the attendance of partici-   5.____
pants.
Such reports are GENERALLY considered to be

    A. an excellent quantitative and qualitative basis for evaluating the success of a pro-
gram
    B. of primary use in operational research involving participant behavior and outcomes
    C. unnecessary since few departments continue to use attendance reports as a basis
for funding
    D. quite inaccurate unless attendance counts are done systematically and staff mem-
bers avoid inflating them

6. An informal survey of recreation in a hospital showed that patients who engaged regu-   6.____
larly in the program were discharged from the hospital earlier than those who did not.
Based on this information only, it would be MOST valid to say that

    A. such information has validity or meaning only to a qualified medical research per-
son
    B. it is inconclusive whether there exists a cause and effect relationship between par-
ticipation and discharge
    C. probably the healthier patients took part in the recreation program, and this was
the reason for their earlier discharge
    D. recreation was the major determinant of earlier discharge

7. The one of the following it would be BEST to do when preparing or developing an annual   7.____
report of a large recreational program is to

    A. gather material such as photos, program descriptions, news stories, and statistics
which appeared during the course of the year
    B. use narrative description rather than charts or graphs to present statistical data
    C. present only the positive aspects and successes of your program, elaborating
when necessary to give a favorable picture
    D. give praise to key political figures in the report so they will support the program in
the future

8. *Crash* programs of recreation have sometimes been rushed into slum areas as a   8.____
response to the threat of violence. Often, the approach has been to present *portable* programs, for example, portable pools put into lots of streets, mobile libraries and nature displays, puppet shows, movies, and rock or soul music shows.
Of the following, the MAJOR weakness of the *portable* recreation approach is that

    A. funds expended for such programs tend to be excessive and the general public is
antagonized
    B. it emphasizes expending aimless energy rather than promoting social growth
    C. it meets only temporary recreation needs and fails to effect a permanent resolution
of recreation problems
    D. it tends to draw large numbers of youth out on the street, where they become riot-
ous

9. A recent change in the concept of recreation as a public service is that it is now being thought of as a kind of social therapy.
The MOST recent illustration of this has been the

    A. joint effort of religious agencies to develop new recreation programs, including year-round camping, for broken families
    B. expanded recreation programs in youth houses, remand institutions, and similar institutions run by the Department of Social Services
    C. new recreation program in private or multi-room occupancy hotels
    D. crash effort to provide recreation programs for alcoholics and older drug addicts

9.____

10. Low-income and racial minority youth tend to have very limited recreation interests. Often, teenage boys want to take part in basketball, but little else of an organized nature.
For a recreation center director, what would be the BEST professional approach to this attitude?

    A. Begin with the interests they already have, then try to broaden their involvement in other recreation, athletic, or cultural activities
    B. Stick to basketball, their true interest, since they resist other activities
    C. Since they are able to play basketball in many neighborhood settings, eliminate this part of the program and offer new kinds of sports, cultural activities, and social events
    D. Rely on carefully prepared interest surveys, and then offer youth only the activities and events they say they want

10.____

11. A NEW trend in many cities, with respect to the assignment of recreation leadership personnel, is to

    A. assign workers to one setting on a full-time, year-round basis so that they will be completely familiar with the work and do a superior job
    B. use seniority more than ever before, thereby giving the long-time employee freedom to pick his job
    C. rotate the assignments of workers from season-to-season or even day-to-day to maximize output and improve morale by giving challenging assignments
    D. create new job shifts, such as one week from 9:00 to 5:00, next week from 2:00 to 10:00, etc.

11.____

12. Recreation counseling is becoming more widely used in many hospitals.
Such counseling is PRIMARILY intended to

    A. help patients explore their leisure attitudes and interests and motivate them toward fuller participation after discharge
    B. teach patients a broad range of activities, such as sports, crafts, and social skills, that they can use after discharge
    C. use the recreation situation to uncover problems that can then be discussed when the patient gets therapeutic counseling
    D. allow the patients to advise staff members on how best to organize the recreation program

12.____

13. A major problem today in many recreation and park departments is costly and destructive vandalism.
    Which of the following methods of dealing with this problem has NOT been widely accepted throughout the United States?

    A. Provide stronger enforcement of rules and better surveillance and protection of recreation and park facilities
    B. Offer more attractive programs since people are less likely to vandalize a facility if it is staffed and providing popular community activities
    C. Use new types of designs so that facilities are less prone to vandalism, such as windowless buildings, concrete benches and tables, etc.
    D. Abandon parks or playgrounds that have been repeatedly vandalized

13.___

14. The Board of Education has a strong commitment to recreation.
    Its recreation program focuses CHIEFLY on

    A. adult education programs in adult centers
    B. children and youth in after-school and evening centers
    C. the categories of pre-school, mentally retarded, and senior citizens
    D. youth either considered to be pre-delinquent or adjudicated as delinquent

14.___

15. Those working to provide recreation to persons who have a physical, mental, emotional, or social disability frequently seek assistance from social service agencies.
    Which of the following pairs of agencies is LEAST likely to be helpful to them?

    A. Catholic Charities; Federation of Protestant Welfare Agencies
    B. United Cerebral Palsy of N.Y.C., Inc.; New York Association for the Blind
    C. New York Association for Retarded Children; National Wheelchair Athletic Association
    D. New York League for Crippled and Disabled Children, Adults and Aging; Handclasp for the Handicapped, Inc.

15.___

16. Throughout the nation, there has been an increase in senior centers for aging persons.
    Which of the following agencies does NOT sponsor special centers for aging persons?

    A. Housing Authority's low-income projects
    B. Office of Continuing Education
    C. Parks, Recreation and Cultural Affairs Administration
    D. Department of Social Services

16.___

17. The municipal department that has the PRIMARY responsibility for providing social services for youth, including recreation, is the

    A. Youth Activities Board
    B. Youth Services Agency
    C. United Block Association for Youth
    D. Bureau of Youth Community Services

17.___

18. If a recreation center director had severe problems with drug users in his neighborhood, the APPROPRIATE municipal department for him to ask for assistance is the

    A. Health and Hospitals Corporation
    B. Synanon or Phoenix House

18.___

C. Department of Correction
D. Addiction Services Agency

Questions 19-20.

DIRECTIONS: Answer Questions 19 and 20 SOLELY on the basis of the following passage.

This country was built on the puritanical belief that honest toil was the foundation of moral rectitude, the cement of society, and the uphill road to progress. Idleness was sin. As a result, we treat free time today as a conditional joy. We permit ourselves to relax only as a reward for hard work or as the recreation needed to put us back into shape for the job. Thus, the aimless delightful play of children gives way in adult life to a serious dedication to golf, the game that is so good for business.

19. According to the passage, during former times in this country, respectable work was considered to be MOST NEARLY a

    A. way to improve health
    B. form of recreation
    C. developer of good character
    D. reward for leisure

19.____

20. According to the point of view presented in the passage, it would be MOST reasonable to assume that an employer would consider an employee's vacation to be a time for the employee to

    A. determine his own leisure time priorities
    B. loaf and relax
    C. learn new recreational skills
    D. increase his effectiveness at work

20.____

Questions 21-23.

DIRECTIONS: Answer Questions 21 through 23 SOLELY on the basis of the following passage.

One of the key supervisory problems in a large municipal recreation department is that many leaders are assigned to isolated playgrounds or small centers, where it is difficult to observe their work regularly. Often their facilities are extremely limited. In such settings, as well as in larger recreation centers, where many recreation leaders tend to have other jobs as well, there tends to be a low level of morale and incentive. Still, it is the supervisor's task to help recreation personnel to develop pride in their work, and to maintain a high level of performance. With isolated leaders, the supervisor may give advice or assistance. Leaders may be assigned to different tasks or settings during the year to maximize their productivity and provide new challenges. When it is clear that leaders are not willing to make a real effort to contribute to the department, the possibility of penalties must be considered, within the scope of departmental policy and the union contract. However, the supervisor should be constructive, encourage and assist workers to take a greater interest in their work, be innovative, and try to raise morale and to improve performance in positive ways.

21. The one of the following that would be the MOST appropriate title for the foregoing passage is 21.___

    A. SMALL COMMUNITY CENTERS - PRO AND CON
    B. PLANNING BETTER RECREATION PROGRAMS
    C. THE SUPERVISOR'S TASK IN UPGRADING PERSONNEL PERFORMANCE
    D. THE SUPERVISOR AND THE MUNICIPAL UNION - RIGHTS AND OBLIGATIONS

22. The passage makes clear that recreation leadership performance in ALL recreation playgrounds and centers throughout a large city is 22.___

    A. generally above average, with good morale on the part of most recreation leaders
    B. beyond description since no one has ever observed or evaluated recreation leaders
    C. a key test of the personnel department's effort to develop more effective hiring standards
    D. of mixed quality, with many recreation leaders having poor morale and a low level of achievement

23. According to the passage, the supervisor's role is to 23.___

    A. use disciplinary action as his major tool in upgrading performance
    B. tolerate the lack of effort of individual employees since they are assigned to isolated playgrounds or small centers
    C. employ encouragement, advice, and, when appropriate, disciplinary action to improve performance
    D. inform the county supervisor whenever malfeasance or idleness is detected

Questions 24-25.

DIRECTIONS: Answer Questions 24 and 25 SOLELY on the basis of the following passage.

A recent study revealed some very concrete evidence concerning the relationship between avocations and mental health. A number of well-adjusted persons were surveyed as to the type, number, and duration of their hobbies. The findings were compared to those from a similar survey of mentally disturbed persons. In the well-adjusted group, both the number of hobbies and the intensity with which they were pursued were far greater than that of the mentally disturbed group.

24. According to the passage, the study showed that 24.___

    A. well-adjusted people engage in hobbies more widely and deeply than do mentally disturbed people
    B. hobbies, if taken seriously, serve to keep most people mentally well
    C. mental patients should be taught hobbies as a part of their therapy
    D. the degree of interest in hobbies plays an important role in maintaining good mental health

25. In reference to the study mentioned in the passage, it is MOST accurate to say that it appears to have   25._____

    A. been based on a carefully-structured, complex research design
    B. considered the variables of mental health and hobby involvement
    C. contained a general definition of mental health
    D. given evidence of a causal relationship between hobbies and mental health

_____

KEY (CORRECT ANSWERS)

1.	D	11.	C
2.	A	12.	A
3.	A	13.	D
4.	D	14.	B
5.	D	15.	D
6.	B	16.	B
7.	A	17.	B
8.	C	18.	D
9.	B	19.	C
10.	A	20.	D

21.	C
22.	D
23.	C
24.	A
25.	B

_____

EXAMINATION SECTION
TEST 1

DIRECTIONS: Each question or incomplete statement is followed by several suggested answers or completions. Select the one that BEST answers the question or completes the statement. *PRINT THE LETTER OF THE CORRECT ANSWER IN THE SPACE AT THE RIGHT.*

1. It has been said, *Leadership, more than areas and facilities, activities, and programs – important as they are – determines the success of municipal recreation service.* The BEST justification of this statement is that

    A. children learn more skills and at a faster rate with good leadership
    B. leadership can make facilities safe
    C. leadership gives deeper significance to the play of children
    D. the program is only as good as the leadership

1.____

2. Changes or progress in our modern society have especially increased the need for recreation facilities of the type which provides

    A. development of friendships
    B. development of teamwork
    C. encouragement to creativeness
    D. individual and group competition

2.____

3. The concept of recreation MOST generally accepted today is the _____ theory.

    A. instinct-practice
    B. recapitulation of culture-epochs
    C. self-expression
    D. surplus-energy

3.____

4. The MOST serious danger of unsupervised play by children is that

    A. children learn many bad habits and acquire prejudices in their play when not supervised
    B. children playing by themselves are subject to greater hazards and potential injury
    C. misdirected play may lead to delinquency
    D. the unsupervised play environment may produce serious frustrations in children

4.____

5. There are certain generally recognized principles of recreation programming for a community.
The FULLEST statement of these principles is:

    A. A recreation plan for the community should result in the fullest use of all resources and be integrated with long-range planning for all other community services.
    B. Education for the worthy use of leisure in homes, schools, and other community institutions is essential.
    C. Opportunities and programs for recreation should be available twelve months of the year.
    D. All of the above

5.____

6. Of the following functions, it is LEAST important for a recreation leader to   6.____

    A. develop a level of skill in children which will enable them to enjoy the activity
    B. develop winning teams
    C. maintain discipline and order
    D. provide opportunity for the greatest number to participate

7. The LEAST accurate of the following statements about the characteristics of a capable   7.____
professional worker in the field of community activities is that he should have the ability to

    A. analyze thoughts and ideas in order to select basic usable concepts
    B. determine for himself, based upon his own professional experience and compe-
tence, the needs of the particular community activity
    C. express warmth of feeling in appropriate ways and without fear, as one basis for a
sound relationship
    D. synthesize out of a mass of associations those which are significant and belong
together in relation to a specific purpose

8. It is a GENERALLY accepted principle that volunteer leaders in a recreation program are   8.____
valuable

    A. as long as they are willing to teach and direct activities without participating in them
    B. despite their need for constant supervision and guidance
    C. if they do not need constant supervision
    D. only if they possess a recreation skill

9. The MOST acceptable definition of discipline, according to the current theory of recre-   9.____
ation, is:

    A. Methods used in special situations to achieve conformance to accepted patterns of
behavior
    B. Punishment for those individuals or groups who violate legitimate rules or regula-
tions which have been established for the general good
    C. The voluntary subordination of the individual to the welfare of the group
    D. Voluntary following of such rules as aid the development and integration of the indi-
vidual

10. Motor skills are fundamental to all sports activity. It is MOST correct to say that motor   10.____
skills

    A. are not generally found among pre-school children
    B. decrease in proportion to the decrease of strength and endurance with age
    C. once learned are never forgotten
    D. reach their highest state of development just after adolescence

11. From the viewpoint of professional recreation philosophy, the suggestion that two boys in   11.____
disagreement should *put on the gloves* is

    A. *desirable;* it is a legitimate way of solving the disagreement
    B. *undesirable;* it assumes that the boy who wins is right in his views
    C. *undesirable;* it ignores the element of safety
    D. *undesirable;* it may involve the city in a lawsuit

12. Of the following, the BEST recreational approach to the problem of reducing juvenile delinquency is:

    A. Make recreational activities more demanding and satisfying than delinquent activities

    B. Provide a well-rounded community activities program and invite potential juvenile delinquents to join

    C. Provide children with a large enough place to play and with proper equipment and they will not get into trouble

    D. There is at present no reliable solution for juvenile delinquency; all we can hope to do is keep the good boys away from the bad

12.____

13. Studies of mental health and interest in hobbies have shown that

    A. interest in hobbies will keep a person mentally well

    B. the mentally well individual is less likely to have an interest in hobbies than the mentally ill person

    C. the mentally well individual is more likely to have an interest in hobbies than the mentally ill person

    D. there is no correlation between the two

13.____

14. The PRINCIPAL use to which a recreation leader should put a knowledge of common children's diseases is to

    A. give occasional advice to parents on safeguarding their children's health

    B. procure a medical history of the child in order to know the activities in which the child may participate

    C. recognize symptoms of conditions which may require medical care

    D. recognize symptoms of contagious diseases which require that a child be separated from the group

14.____

15. A child falls from a tree, hitting his head on the pavement below, knocking himself unconscious.
The BEST first aid measures to take are:

    A. Apply a pressure bandage to prevent any bleeding and do not move the patient until the doctor arrives

    B. Avoid unnecessary handling and administer a mild stimulant when the child becomes conscious

    C. Do not move the patient but cover him with a coat or blanket until the doctor arrives

    D. Do not move the patient until the doctor arrives unless the patient demonstrates unusual lucidity and energy when he returns to consciousness

15.____

16. A thorough investigation should always be made of any accident occurring in a Park Department playground.
The MAIN value of such an investigation is to

    A. demonstrate to the parents the interest which the Park Department takes in the care and safety of the children

    B. discover any factors that may be corrected which contributed to the accident

16.____

C. establish the extent to which Park Department employees may be responsible for the accident

D. provide a record of the accident so that the facts may be available in the event of a lawsuit

17. The MOST important of the following principles to consider in selecting games for a group is: 17.___

   A. Games should be adapted to the age-range, the number of members, and the various factors of difference represented in the group

   B. Games should be selected which are related to the cultural and ethnic backgrounds of the participants

   C. Games should not be complicated to teach, score, or perform

   D. The previous recreational experience of the participants should form the basis of selection

18. It is a common practice for playgrounds to conduct special events or celebrations at certain times. 18.___
The MOST important principle which should guide planners of these events is:

   A. The regular program of the playground should be suspended, if necessary, in order to provide ample opportunity for practice

   B. They should be an outgrowth of the regular playground program

   C. They require much planning; hence, they should be scheduled at least six months in advance

   D. They should seldom be financed from the playground budget, but rather an outside sponsor should be sought

19. In basketball, when playing against a zone defense, the BEST strategy is 19.___

   A. set up weak side plays by overloading one side

   B. use a fast break

   C. use more dribbling than you would against a man-to-man defense

   D. utilize screens, quick cuts, and criss-cross breaks

20. In volleyball, the MOST effective method of passing, taking into account both control and power, is by having the 20.___

   A. arm kept rigid, the ball in direct contact with the palm of the hand, and snapping the wrist in the direction of the flight

   B. the fingers in contact with the ball, swinging the arm with a lifting motion

   C. heel of the hand in firm contact with the ball, swinging the arm with a lifting motion

   D. palm of the hand in direct contact with the ball, swinging the arm with a lifting motion

21. Generally speaking, it is good technique in batting in the game of softball to 21.___

   A. select a bat that feels rather heavy

   B. swing at all balls that come within reach

   C. swing the bat so that it is parallel to the ground at the moment of impact

   D. swing with all your might at the ball

22. The one of the following which is a rule of handball doubles is:　　22.____

    A. A game is 25 points
    B. A *hinder* is called if a player drives a ball into an opponent and a point is credited to the side of the man who was hit
    C. If one partner swings at the ball and misses, the other partner is permitted to return the ball
    D. To keep the ball in play, it must be struck after hitting the wall and before hitting the ground

23. The activity which is especially useful with a large, cumbersome group of untutored individuals, as a lead-up activity to the production of a play, is　　23.____

    A. answer-back story
    B. Blackout
    C. Little Tom Tinker
    D. puppet show

24. Analysis of the motion of a schottische dance shows the following sequence of fundamental steps:　　24.____

    A. High brush step to the right side, close and transfer of weight left, and a hop left
    B. Step, step, close
    C. Three small runs followed by a hop
    D. Two hops, step, close, step

25. In recommending the purchase of playground equipment, a guiding principle should be that　　25.____

    A. durability is usually at least as important as suitability
    B. equipment should be bought with a view to serving the largest number of participants
    C. good equipment, carefully selected, can largely substitute for leadership
    D. small areas should be loaded with apparatus

26. In introducing a game to a group unfamiliar with it, it is LEAST important that　　26.____

    A. introductory instructions be brief
    B. the game be a simple one
    C. the game be stopped while interest is still high
    D. the leader assume a confident, positive approach

27. When starting a new craft program, it is IMPORTANT that the leader　　27.____

    A. employ much technical vocabulary unfamiliar to most members of the group in order to establish his expert status
    B. exclude from the group anyone whose skill in the craft is superior to the leader so as to prevent dual leadership
    C. start with material familiar to most members of the group so as to build confidence in their ability to absorb what is to come
    D. treat the group as homogeneous, disregarding individual differences

28. The one of the following which BEST expresses a desirable characteristic of group lead-   28.___
    ership is:

    A. Advises the group as to suitable objectives and means of accomplishing them;
    assists in settling disagreements arising within the group

    B. Arranges effective intercommunication among the group; does not permit any con-
    flicts to arise

    C. Permits the members of the group to set its own objectives and the means of
    accomplishing them; does not intercede to resolve conflicts

    D. Sets proper objectives of the group and instructs in the correct method of accom-
    plishing those objectives; settles any disputes that may arise

Questions 29-43.

DIRECTIONS: Column I lists a series of activities numbered from 29 through 43, each of
which is to be matched with one of the choices given in Column II. For each
item of Column I, write in the space at the right the letter in front of the choice
in Column II with which it is MOST closely related.

COLUMN I	COLUMN II	
29. Bait casting	A. Allemande	29. ___
	B. Awl	
30. Block printing	C. Batik	30. ___
	D. Blue-tail Fly	
31. Circle game	E. Egg balancing	31. ___
	F. Ghost	
32. Dramatics	G. Kiln	32. ___
	H. Linoleum	
33. Finger painting	I. Loop Tennis	33. ___
	J. Miming	
34. Folk song	K. Miter box	34. ___
35. Handicraft with cloth	L. Mumblety-peg	35. ___
	M. Newcomb	
36. Leather craft	N. Over and Under	36. ___
	O. Puck	
37. Nature study	P. Skishing	37. ___
	Q. Soap flakes and starch	
38. Net game	R. Terrarium	38. ___
39. Pottery craft	S. Three Deep	39. ___
	T. Titanium	
40. Relay game	U. Wicket	40. ___
41. Square dance		41. ___
42. Woodworking		42. ___
43. Word game		43. ___

44. In dealing with an individual who displays his insecurity by aggressive behavior, the group leader should FIRST

    44._____

    A. directly champion the individual to the group
    B. indicate acceptance of the individual by the leader
    C. insist that the individual withdraw from the group for a temporary period
    D. permit the group to attempt to deal with the individual

45. Studies of clubs and gangs have indicated certain basic facts about them. The one of the following which is NOT a basic characteristic of clubs or gangs is:

    45._____

    A. Participation in either street gangs or street clubs is a part of the growing up process of some adolescents
    B. Repressive measures in dealing with antisocial behavior of clubs or gangs brings about basic changes in attitudes and behavior
    C. Some clubs or gangs, as a result of fundamental factors such as poor housing, racial discrimination, or emotional maladjustment of their leaders or members, have developed patterns of antisocial behavior
    D. To be effective in modifying antisocial behavior of clubs or gangs, it is imperative that a social worker be assigned to only one street club or gang

46. A basketball team in a community center was composed of a group of boys who were inseparable in most of their free time. The group became involved in some antisocial activities because the most vocal and influential members of the group were able to persuade some of the other boys who individually would not have committed the wrong acts. This latter minority was PROBABLY involved because the

    46._____

    A. community center had failed to break up the team so that the delinquent boys would not have had a chance to corrupt the non-delinquent
    B. community center had failed to sublimate the adolescent's need for adventure
    C. members of the group were inherently delinquentprone
    D. need to belong to the group was so great that some boys agreed to behavior which was actually unacceptable to them

47. Hostile feelings held by a few members of an organized group are LEAST likely to be reduced by

    47._____

    A. appointing a committee to deal with the problem, with the disgruntled ones made members of the committee
    B. holding group discussions of the reasons for the hostility
    C. insisting upon the will of the majority
    D. making concessions to the hostile group

48. Of the following statements concerning groups, it is MOST correct to say:

    48._____

    A. Hostile feelings are wrong and must be weeded out
    B. Signs of hostility prove the group was poorly chosen
    C. So long as hostile feelings are felt with equal strength by every member of a group, the group will function efficiently together
    D. The need to be together subordinates hostile feelings

49. The one of the following agencies which has initial jurisdiction over children apprehended 49.___
by the Police Department is the

    A. City Youth Board
    C. Juvenile Aid Bureau
    B. Family Court
    D. Youth Bureau

50. The one of the following which BEST characterizes the philosophy of the City Youth 50.___
Board is:

    A. Reform the gang; efforts to improve individuals as such have proved fruitless
    B. Search for the child in need; do not wait for the child to express a willingness to
       accept help
    C. Work through the children; the children will reform the parents
    D. Work through the parents; they will teach their children what is right

KEY (CORRECT ANSWERS)

1.	C	11.	B	21.	C	31.	S	41.	A
2.	C	12.	A	22.	C	32.	J	42.	K
3.	C	13.	C	23.	A	33.	Q	43.	F
4.	B	14.	D	24.	C	34.	D	44.	B
5.	D	15.	C	25.	B	35.	C	45.	B
6.	B	16.	B	26.	B	36.	B	46.	D
7.	B	17.	A	27.	C	37.	R	47.	C
8.	B	18.	B	28.	A	38.	M	48.	D
9.	C	19.	A	29.	P	39.	G	49.	C
10.	C	20.	B	30.	H	40.	N	50.	B

TEST 2

DIRECTIONS: Each question or incomplete statement is followed by several suggested answers or completions. Select the one that BEST answers the question or completes the statement. *PRINT THE LETTER OF THE CORRECT ANSWER IN THE SPACE AT THE RIGHT.*

1. The GREATEST value to the playground program in having an effective public relations program is that it

    1._____

    A. creates public appreciation of the professional nature of recreation work
    B. encourages participation
    C. helps to interpret the program and solicit support for it
    D. is the most effective means of assuring administrative approval of a satisfactory budget

2. In handling publicity for a recreation program, it is BEST to

    2._____

    A. allow public demand to govern the rate at which information is given them
    B. coordinate all publicity with special outstanding recreational events
    C. intensify publicity efforts whenever the public loses interest
    D. maintain constant flow of information to the public at all times

3. Of the following, the MOST important reason for the professional staff in a community center to keep detailed records of an organized group is the contribution the record makes toward

    3._____

    A. better understanding of individuals and the group as a whole
    B. effective program planning for the entire center
    C. proper selection of participants for tournaments or festivals
    D. interpreting the services of the program to the public

4. Of the following, the MOST important reason for part-time workers in a community center to keep detailed records of organized groups is the contribution the record makes toward

    4._____

    A. interpreting the services of the program to the public
    B. effective program planning for the entire center
    C. proper selection of participants for tournaments or festivals
    D. providing continuity of information in the event that group leadership changes

5. The GENERAL purposes for which staff meetings of recreation personnel should be called are share experiences and problems,

    5._____

    A. reprimand the inefficient, prepare plans, and coordinate effort
    B. evaluate activities and services, explain new sports and activities, and coordinate effort
    C. evaluate activities and services, prepare plans, and coordinate effort
    D. evaluate activities and services, prepare plans, and introduce new members of the staff

6. In planning the conduct of a staff meeting to be called for the purpose of solving a partic-   6.___
ular problem, the one of the following which should occur after all the others is the

    A. adoption of a plan of action
    B. definite allocation of responsibility
    C. discussion of the problem by the supervisor
    D. exchange of opinions

7. At a staff conference, one member of the staff frequently has good ideas but he   7.___
expresses them poorly.
It would be BEST for the supervisor to

    A. disregard the manner in which the ideas are presented
    B. permit the staff member to express his ideas and for the supervisor to rephrase the
ideas presented in a more readily understandable manner
    C. postpone consideration of these ideas to the next conference so that the staff
member can put his ideas in clearer and better form
    D. suggest that the staff member explain his ideas to the supervisor before the staff
meeting so that the supervisor may present the ideas at the meeting in a more
readily understandable manner

8. The method of allowing news of forthcoming changes in policy to be spread by rumor   8.___
and other unofficial means is

    A. *bad,* because it detracts from the status of the lower level supervisors
    B. *bad,* because newly appointed employees will not get the necessary information
    C. *good,* because it permits changes to be made in the policy before its official
announcement in response to valid objections which may be expressed
    D. *good,* because it results in the most rapid dissemination of information about the
new policy

9. Prestige is a factor which, consciously or unconsciously, is considered by most supervi-   9.___
sors to be important.
From the point of view of good management, enhancing the prestige of a supervisor is

    A. *bad,* because it builds up the supervisor's importance without equally achieving the
aims of management
    B. *good,* as a measure of economy since it may serve as a substitute for increased
salary
    C. *good,* because it increases the supervisor's identification with, and support of,
management aims
    D. *good,* in order to build the subordinates' awareness of, and belief in, the supervi-
sor's authority

10. A desirable characteristic of a good supervisor is that he should   10.___

    A. identify himself with his subordinates rather than with higher management
    B. inform subordinates of forthcoming changes in policies and programs only when
they directly affect the subordinates' activities
    C. make advancement of the subordinates contingent on personal loyalty to the
supervisor
    D. make promises to subordinates only when sure of the ability to keep them

11. The supervisor who is MOST likely to be successful is the one who   11._____

    A.   refrains from exercising the special privileges of his position
    B.   maintains a formal attitude toward his subordinates
    C.   maintains an informal attitude toward his subordinates
    D.   represents the desires of his subordinates to his superiors

12. Application of sound principles of human relations by a supervisor may be expected to   12._____
    _____ the need for formal discipline.

    A.   decrease   B.   have no effect on
    C.   increase   D.   obviate

13. The MOST important generally approved way to maintain or develop high morale in   13._____
    one's subordinates is to

    A.   give warnings and reprimands in a jocular manner
    B.   excuse from staff conferences those employees who are busy
    C.   keep them informed of new developments and policies of higher management
    D.   refrain from criticizing their faults directly

14. In training subordinates, an important principle for the supervisor to recognize is that   14._____

    A.   a particular method of instruction will be of substantially equal value for all employ-
         ees in a given title
    B.   it is difficult to train people over 50 years of age because they have little capacity
         for learning
    C.   persons undergoing the same course of training will learn at different rates of
         speed
    D.   training can seldom achieve its purpose unless individual instruction is the chief
         method used

15. Over an extended period of time, a subordinate is MOST likely to become and remain   15._____
    most productive if the supervisor

    A.   accords praise to the subordinate whenever his work is satisfactory, withholding
         criticism except in the case of very inferior work
    B.   avoids both praise and criticism except for outstandingly good or bad work per-
         formed by the subordinate
    C.   informs the subordinate of his shortcomings, as viewed by management, while
         according praise only when highly deserved
    D.   keeps the subordinate informed of the degree of satisfaction with which his perfor-
         mance of the job is viewed by management

16. A playground director has not properly carried out the orders of his assistant supervisor   16._____
    of recreation on several occasions to the point where he has been successively warned,
    reprimanded, and severely reprimanded. When the playground director once again does
    not carry out orders, the PROPER action for the assistant supervisor of recreation to take
    is to

    A.   bring the playground director up on charges of failing to perform his duties properly
    B.   have a serious discussion with the playground director explaining the need for the
         orders and the necessity for carrying them out

C. recommend that the playground director be transferred to another district
D. severely reprimand the playground director again, making clear that no further deviation will be countenanced

17. A supervisor with several subordinates becomes aware that two of these subordinates are neither friendly nor congenial.
In making assignments, it would be BEST for the supervisor to

    17.____

A. disregard the situation
B. disregard the situation in making a choice of assignment but emphasize the need for teamwork
C. investigate the situation to find out who is at fault, and give that individual the less desirable assignments until such time as he corrects his attitude
D. place the unfriendly subordinates in positions where they have as little contact with one another as possible

18. A group of newly appointed recreation leaders have been assigned to your jurisdiction. Of the following, the MOST important thing for you to do when they report for work on their first day is to

    18.____

A. assign them to definite areas of responsibility
B. describe to them sickness, absence, and vacation policies
C. discuss with them the social philosophy of public recreation
D. inform them of the general character and duties of the job

19. Assume that a new procedure in the conduct of tournaments has been adopted which you, as supervisor, think may meet with staff resistance.
To accomplish the general aims of supervision and to minimize any anticipated resistance to the new procedure, it would be BEST to

    19.____

A. approach the members of the staff individually and, on a personal basis, gain their promise of cooperation
B. explain the reason for the new procedure at a staff meeting and advise the staff that they must accept it regardless of their personal feelings
C. elect or appoint a staff committee to study and report on the advantages and disadvantages of the new procedure
D. issue detailed instructions on the use of the new procedure to facilitate its application

20. When you become aware that a recreation leader under your supervision has failed to follow the proper procedure in certain cases and has concealed the fact that he has failed to do so, it would be BEST for you to

    20.____

A. discuss with him both the error and the reason for its concealment, with the aim of improving the relationship between superior and subordinate
B. explain the proper procedure to him and reprimand him for having concealed his failure to follow it
C. make no mention of the matter but supervise him more closely in the future
D. tell him that the proper procedure must be followed since failure to do so is a violation of the rules of the department

21. One of the basic objectives of recreation is satisfaction or enjoyment.
The one of the following which contributes LEAST to the accomplishment of this objective is

    A. being accepted and wanted by others of the same age
    B. complete escape through an interesting and all-consuming activity
    C. recognition from others by applause or praise
    D. receiving material recognition for effort

21.____

22. In discussing public schools and public recreation centers, recreation leaders have
agreed that

    A. education is not an important aim of public recreation
    B. in both areas, education for the worthy use of leisure is essential
    C. motivation for learning is greater in public schools than in recreation centers
    D. the methods of teaching are the same in the two areas

22.____

23. The one of the following which the recreation leader is LEAST expected to develop in
children participating in a playground program is

    A. acceptance of the rules of the game or activity
    B. cooperation with other children
    C. respect for the equipment being used
    D. skill in the activity

23.____

24. Using the family, rather than the individual, as the central unit in the development of a
public recreation program is

    A. *desirable* but expensive to operate
    B. *undesirable* and expensive to operate
    C. *desirable* because it is inexpensive to operate
    D. *undesirable* except for the saving in operating expenses

24.____

25. In thinking of juvenile delinquency prevention, the MOST limited and narrow approach to
prevention would stress

    A. improving all aspects of life that affect children's social, moral, religious, educa-
tional, and physical growth
    B. promoting healthy personality development of all children
    C. reducing recidivism should take priority over reaching children not yet law violators
    D. reaching that segment which predictive signs indicate are the potential delinquents

25.____

26. In starting a recreational program for people over sixty-five years of age, it is of FIRST
importance to provide

    A. arts and crafts equipment and supplies
    B. a sense of belonging
    C. leadership and remove taxing responsibility
    D. very comfortable surroundings

26.____

27. In preparing a program of games, physical strength and stamina of the expected participants must be considered. When preparing a program for a group of 10-year-olds, it should be remembered that the girls of this age are
    27.____

    A. as strong and active as boys of the same age
    B. more physically mature than boys of the same age
    C. passing through a period of physical weakness
    D. weaker and have less stamina than boys of the same age in all probability

28. In conducting a party for children in the eight to twelve year age group, it is LEAST important that
    28.____

    A. children understand that controls on wild behavior exist
    B. instructions for games be brief and entertaining
    C. the games involve all of the children at once
    D. there be several games in which girls and boys form partnerships

29. The MOST desirable means of attracting children under ten years of age to the recreation center is to conduct a special event such as a
    29.____

    A. costume parade   B. field day
    C. marbles tournament   D. song contest

30. In laying out a playground to serve a highly populated urban area, it is BEST to
    30.____

    A. eliminate landscaping and arrangements that consume space
    B. make use of all available space even at the expense of not grouping activity areas by age level or degree of required supervision
    C. provide for multiple use of many play areas
    D. revise standard dimensions of sports diamonds and courts to enable the inclusion of an unusually large variety of activities

31. Of the following, the MOST important consideration in planning a playground site for children 4 to 6 years of age is
    31.____

    A. confining fence or hedge
    B. grassy area
    C. hard surface area (such as asphalt)
    D. plenty of shade

32. Registration of participants as a tool for evaluating the effectiveness of a recreation program is
    32.____

    A. a procedure receiving increasing acceptance for use with all activities
    B. generally too cumbersome a procedure to be of any value
    C. of value only when no attendance counts are made
    D. practical for use with many activities but impractical for use with many other activities

33. Special events are considered a desirable aspect of any playground program CHIEFLY because they
    33.____

    A. add variety and a change of pace to the program
    B. are incentives to participants

C. are one of the best ways to terminate a seasonal program
D. have tremendous public relations value

34. One of the basic reasons why it is important for group leaders to focus on individual and group objectives is that doing so   34._____

    A. guarantees a better planned schedule of activities
    B. insures a fairer process in program planning
    C. reduces the likelihood that the group's individual needs will be the basis for program planning
    D. reduces the likelihood that the leader's own individual needs will be the basis on which the groups' program is determined

35. Recreation changes in character and emphasis from one age group to another. It is MOST characteristic of the pre-school child as compared with older children that the pre-school child   35._____

    A. likes to play with others
    B. likes vigorous games
    C. plays very much by himself
    D. possesses a group spirit

36. When members of two racial groups participate in common social and recreational activities, the MOST likely effect on racial prejudice is to   36._____

    A. increase the prejudice
    B. decrease the prejudice
    C. either increase it or decrease it, depending upon the effective leadership of the groups
    D. have no effect upon the prejudice

37. Among the regular users of a community recreation center are two well-defined groups, organized on a racial basis, which have little or no contact with each other.
An attempt to dispel the existing racial prejudice may BEST be made by organizing a center-wide   37._____

    A. dance requiring cooperative action by both groups for planning and preparations
    B. party requiring cooperative action by both groups for planning and preparation
    C. dance to be sponsored and conducted by one group and to which the other group will be invited
    D. party to be sponsored and conducted by one group and to which the other group will be invited

38. The one of the following which is NOT a basic principle governing the successful operation of a teen center is: 38._____

    A. The closing time should not be too late, about 10 P.M.
    B. Separate problems should be set up for the young teenagers and for the older teenagers
    C. The center should be open whenever it will be patronized by a sizable group of teenagers
    D. The center should remain open during school holidays and vacation times

39. When a newly appointed recreation leader requests advice from an assistant supervisor of recreation on the proper way to handle several disruptive but not disturbed children who frequent the playground to which he has been assigned, the assistant supervisor of recreation should suggest that the recreation leader

    39.____

    A.   exclude the children from the playground since they are a disruptive influence
    B.   include the children in activities and accord them special recognition
    C.   make his own decisions since he knows the children best
    D.   refer the children to a psychiatric clinic for help in achieving proper social adjustment

40. By a majority vote, after full discussion and participation, the members of a teenage canteen agreed upon a set of regulations. A minority threatened to withdraw from the canteen if the rules were enforced.
The principle to be recognized in this situation is:

    40.____

    A.   The rules probably were too stringent and should be revised so that the minority will have its rights preserved
    B.   The basic aims of democracy are not violated if we insist upon conformity once the rules have been agreed upon
    C.   The basic aims of democracy are violated if we insist upon conformity once the rules have been agreed upon
    D.   The basic aims of democracy require that this decision be vetoed in the interests of the minority

41. A community center program for teenagers has been criticized because the participants do not get home until several hours after the center closed.
In such a situation, it is BEST that the center director

    41.____

    A.   advise the parents that he can do nothing about the time their children arrive home because he has no control over the children after they leave the center
    B.   confer with the parents and with the teenagers to establish a home arrival time acceptable to community mores
    C.   extend the closing time of the center to conform with the hour that the teenagers usually get home
    D.   warn the teenagers that the program will be discontinued unless they go home within a short time after the closing of the center

42. It is of importance for a teen center to use a substantial part of its funds to arouse and maintain interest among a high proportion of its potential and active members.
This objective is MOST likely to be accomplished by

    42.____

    A.   arranging for sweaters, pins, or other emblems with the name of the center emblazoned on it to be distributed to all members at a nominal charge
    B.   careful planning to provide a wide range of activities
    C.   operating on a *come and go* basis
    D.   restricting the program to providing a meeting and lounging place, conducting dances, sponsoring parties, and providing opportunities for certain games

43. The organization of neighborhood recreation councils or committees should be encouraged by an assistant supervisor of recreation CHIEFLY because such councils or committees can

    A. help plan the recreation program and promote public interest in it in the neighborhood
    B. help train volunteer leaders
    C. sponsor tournaments and pageants
    D. supervise and evaluate the existing recreation programs in terms of community needs

43.____

44. The MOST valid means of evaluating the effectiveness of a program of recreation or informal education is

    A. appraisal of community support for the program as evidenced by Community Chest support (for private agencies) or tax support (for public services)
    B. appraisal of the program's purposes and performance in the light of community-wide conditions, needs, and services
    C. documented testimony of its value given by those who have participated in the program
    D. participation in the program by a substantial majority of the community

44.____

45. The author of A PHILOSOPHY OF RECREATION AND LEISURE is

    A. Bancroft   B. Butler   C. Meyer   D. Nash

45.____

46. An assistant supervisor of recreation should recognize that the training of recreation leaders is

    A. never complete, and they require continual additional training and instruction
    B. seldom complete until they have received practical on-the-job training
    C. substantially complete once they have been broken in on the job, except for the need for occasional refresher courses
    D. substantially complete at the time they are appointed since they are professional trained people

46.____

47. If a supervisor realizes that he has mistakenly blamed one of his subordinates for a certain situation, it would be BEST for the supervisor to

    A. apologize to the subordinate at the next staff meeting
    B. apologize to the subordinate at the first opportunity
    C. ignore the occurrence
    D. make no mention of the mistake but act more favorably toward the subordinate as an indication that he has realized his error

47.____

48. If a subordinate requests a transfer to a job in another division, a job of no greater apparent value to the department and no greater value to the subordinate, it would be BEST for the supervisor to

    A. recommend the transfer only if the employee can give a good reason for wanting it
    B. refer the matter to his superior without recommendation

48.____

C. refuse the transfer on the grounds that it is not in the best interest of the department

D. request the employee to explain why he wants the transfer before recommending it

49. In teaching a new job to an employee, the MOST frequent of the following sources of difficulty is the

    49.____

    A. desire of the employee to do the job in his own way
    B. incompatibility of personalities of teacher and pupil
    C. lack of confidence of the employee in his ability to learn
    D. unwillingness of the employee to learn something new

50. At a staff meeting of your division, you intend to present a new plan which you have devised.
It is MOST important for you to

    50.____

    A. anticipate objections and be prepared to answer them
    B. be able to demonstrate clearly the value of the plan in your own particular area of responsibility
    C. be prepared to scrap the plan if you encounter strong opposition
    D. prepare the plan so that it will probably be accepted without alteration

_____

KEY (CORRECT ANSWERS)

1. C	11. D	21. D	31. A	41. B
2. D	12. A	22. B	32. D	42. B
3. A	13. C	23. C	33. B	43. A
4. D	14. C	24. A	34. D	44. B
5. C	15. D	25. C	35. C	45. D
6. B	16. A	26. B	36. C	46. A
7. B	17. D	27. A	37. B	47. B
8. A	18. D	28. D	38. A	48. D
9. D	19. B	29. A	39. B	49. C
10. D	20. A	30. C	40. B	50. A

_____

RECORD KEEPING
EXAMINATION SECTION
TEST 1

DIRECTIONS: Each question or incomplete statement is followed by several suggested answers or completions. Select the one that BEST answers the question or completes the statement. *PRINT THE LETTER OF THE CORRECT ANSWER IN THE SPACE AT THE RIGHT.*

Questions 1-15.

DIRECTIONS: Questions 1 through 15 are to be answered on the basis of the following list of company names below. Arrange a file alphabetically, word-by-word, disregarding punctuation, conjunctions, and apostrophes. Then answer the questions.

A Bee C Reading Materials
ABCO Parts
A Better Course for Test Preparation
AAA Auto Parts Co.
A-Z Auto Parts, Inc.
Aabar Books
Abbey, Joanne
Boman-Sylvan Law Firm
BMW Autowerks
C Q Service Company
Chappell-Murray, Inc.
E&E Life Insurance
Emcrisco
Gigi Arts
Gordon, Jon & Associates
SOS Plumbing
Schmidt, J.B. Co.

1. Which of these files should appear FIRST?   1.____

   A. ABCO Parts
   B. A Bee C Reading Materials
   C. A Better Course for Test Preparation
   D. AAA Auto Parts Co.

2. Which of these files should appear SECOND?   2.____

   A. A-Z Auto Parts, Inc.
   B. A Bee C Reading Materials
   C. A Better Course for Test Preparation
   D. AAA Auto Parts Co.

3. Which of these files should appear THIRD?   3.____

   A. ABCO Parts
   B. A Bee C Reading Materials
   C. Aabar Books
   D. AAA Auto Parts Co.

4. Which of these files should appear FOURTH?   4.____

   A. Aabar Books
   B. ABCO Parts
   C. Abbey, Joanne
   D. AAA Auto Parts Co.

5. Which of these files should appear LAST?   5.____

   A. Gordon, Jon & Associates
   B. Gigi Arts
   C. Schmidt, J.B. Co.
   D. SOS Plumbing

6. Which of these files should appear between A-Z Auto Parts, Inc. and Abbey, Joanne?   6.____

   A. A Bee C Reading Materials
   B. AAA Auto Parts Co.
   C. ABCO Parts
   D. A Better Course for Test Preparation

7. Which of these files should appear between ABCO Parts and Aabar Books?   7.____

   A. A Bee C Reading Materials
   B. Abbey, Joanne
   C. Aabar Books
   D. A-Z Auto Parts

8. Which of these files should appear between Abbey, Joanne and Boman-Sylvan Law Firm?   8.____

   A. A Better Course for Test Preparation
   B. BMW Autowerks
   C. Chappell-Murray, Inc.
   D. Aabar Books

9. Which of these files should appear between Abbey, Joanne and C Q Service?   9.____

   A. A-Z Auto Parts,Inc.   B. BMW Autowerks
   C. Choices A and B   D. Chappell-Murray, Inc.

10. Which of these files should appear between C Q Service Company and Emcrisco?   10.____

   A. Chappell-Murray, Inc.   B. E&E Life Insurance
   C. Gigi Arts   D. Choices A and B

11. Which of these files should NOT appear between C Q Service Company and E&E Life Insurance?   11.____

   A. Gordon, Jon & Associates
   B. Emcrisco
   C. Gigi Arts
   D. All of the above

12. Which of these files should appear between Chappell-Murray Inc., and Gigi Arts?   12.____

     A.   CQ Service Inc. E&E Life Insurance, and Emcrisco
     B.   Emcrisco, E&E Life Insurance, and Gordon, Jon & Associates
     C.   E&E Life Insurance and Emcrisco
     D.   Emcrisco and Gordon, Jon & Associates

13. Which of these files should appear between Gordon, Jon & Associates and SOS Plumbing?   13.____

     A.   Gigi Arts   B.   Schmidt, J.B. Co.
     C.   Choices A and B   D.   None of the above

14. Each of the choices lists the four files in their proper alphabetical order except   14.____

     A.   E&E Life Insurance; Gigi Arts; Gordon, Jon & Associates; SOS Plumbing
     B.   E&E Life Insurance; Emcrisco; Gigi Arts; SOS Plumbing
     C.   Emcrisco; Gordon, Jon & Associates; SOS Plumbing; Schmidt, J.B. Co.
     D.   Emcrisco; Gigi Arts; Gordon, Jon & Associates; SOS Plumbing

15. Which of the choices lists the four files in their proper alphabetical order?   15.____

     A.   Gigi Arts; Gordon, Jon & Associates; SOS Plumbing; Schmidt, J.B. Co.
     B.   Gordon, Jon & Associates; Gigi Arts; Schmidt, J.B. Co.; SOS Plumbing
     C.   Gordon, Jon & Associates; Gigi Arts; SOS Plumbing; Schmidt, J.B. Co.
     D.   Gigi Arts; Gordon, Jon & Associates; Schmidt, J.B. Co.; SOS Plumbing

16. The alphabetical filing order of two businesses with identical names is determined by the   16.____

     A.   length of time each business has been operating
     B.   addresses of the businesses
     C.   last name of the company president
     D.   none of the above

17. In an alphabetical filing system, if a business name includes a number, it should be   17.____

     A.   disregarded
     B.   considered a number and placed at the end of an alphabetical section
     C.   treated as though it were written in words and alphabetized accordingly
     D.   considered a number and placed at the beginning of an alphabetical section

18. If a business name includes a contraction (such as *don't* or *it's*), how should that word be treated in an alphabetical filing system?   18.____

     A.   Divide the word into its separate parts and treat it as two words.
     B.   Ignore the letters that come after the apostrophe.
     C.   Ignore the word that contains the contraction.
     D.   Ignore the apostrophe and consider all letters in the contraction.

19. In what order should the parts of an address be considered when using an alphabetical filing system?   19.____

     A.   City or town; state; street name; house or building number
     B.   State; city or town; street name; house or building number
     C.   House or building number; street name; city or town; state
     D.   Street name; city or town; state

20. A business record should be cross-referenced when a(n) 20.___

    A. organization is known by an abbreviated name
    B. business has a name change because of a sale, incorporation, or other reason
    C. business is known by a *coined* or common name which differs from a dictionary spelling
    D. all of the above

21. A geographical filing system is MOST effective when 21.___

    A. location is more important than name
    B. many names or titles sound alike
    C. dealing with companies who have offices all over the world
    D. filing personal and business files

Questions 22-25.

DIRECTIONS: Questions 22 through 25 are to be answered on the basis of the list of items below, which are to be filed geographically. Organize the items geographically and then answer the questions.

    1. University Press at Berkeley, U.S.
    2. Maria Sanchez, Mexico City, Mexico
    3. Great Expectations Ltd. in London, England
    4. Justice League, Cape Town, South Africa, Africa
    5. Crown Pearls Ltd. in London, England
    6. Joseph Prasad in London, England

22. Which of the following arrangements of the items is composed according to the policy of: 22.___
Continent, Country, City, Firm or Individual Name?

    A. 5, 3, 4, 6, 2, 1   B. 4, 5, 3, 6, 2, 1
    C. 1, 4, 5, 3, 6, 2   D. 4, 5, 3, 6, 1, 2

23. Which of the following files is arranged according to the policy of: *Continent, Country,* 23.___
City, Firm or Individual Name?

    A. South Africa. Africa. Cape Town. Justice League
    B. Mexico. Mexico City, Maria Sanchez
    C. North America. United States. Berkeley. University Press
    D. England. Europe. London. Prasad, Joseph

24. Which of the following arrangements of the items is composed according to the policy of: 24.___
Country, City, Firm or Individual Name?

    A. 5, 6, 3, 2, 4, 1   B. 1, 5, 6, 3, 2, 4
    C. 6, 5, 3, 2, 4, 1   D. 5, 3, 6, 2, 4, 1

25. Which of the following files is arranged according to a policy of: *Country, City, Firm or* 25.___
Individual Name?

    A. England. London. Crown Pearls Ltd.
    B. North America. United States. Berkeley. University Press
    C. Africa. Cape Town. Justice League
    D. Mexico City. Mexico. Maria Sanchez

26. Under which of the following circumstances would a phonetic filing system be MOST effective?   26._____

    A. When the person in charge of filing can't spell very well
    B. With large files with names that sound alike
    C. With large files with names that are spelled alike
    D. All of the above

Questions 27-29.

DIRECTIONS: Questions 27 through 29 are to be answered on the basis of the following list of numerical files.
    1. 391-023-100
    2. 361-132-170
    3. 385-732-200
    4. 381-432-150
    5. 391-632-387
    6. 361-423-303
    7. 391-123-271

27. Which of the following arrangements of the files follows a consecutive-digit system?   27._____

    A. 2, 3, 4, 1   B. 1, 5, 7, 3
    C. 2, 4, 3, 1   D. 3, 1, 5, 7

28. Which of the following arrangements follows a terminal-digit system?   28._____

    A. 1, 7, 2, 4, 3   B. 2, 1, 4, 5, 7
    C. 7, 6, 5, 4, 3   D. 1, 4, 2, 3, 7

29. Which of the following lists follows a middle-digit system?   29._____

    A. 1, 7, 2, 6, 4, 5, 3   B. 1, 2, 7, 4, 6, 5, 3
    C. 7, 2, 1, 3, 5, 6, 4   D. 7, 1, 2, 4, 6, 5, 3

Questions 30-31.

DIRECTIONS: Questions 30 and 31 are to be answered on the basis of the following information.
    1. Reconfirm Laura Bates appointment with James Caldecort on December 12 at 9:30 A.M.
    2. Laurence Kinder contact Julia Lucas on August 3 and set up a meeting for week of September 23 at 4 P.M.
    3. John Lutz contact Larry Waverly on August 3 and set up appointment for September 23 at 9:30 A.M.
    4. Call for tickets for Gerry Stanton August 21 for New Jersey on September 23, flight 143 at 4:43 P.M.

30. A chronological file for the above information would be 30.____

    A. 4, 3, 2, 1   B. 3, 2, 4, 1
    C. 4, 2, 3, 1   D. 3, 1, 2, 4

31. Using the above information, a chronological file for the date of September 23 would be   31.____

    A. 2, 3, 4   B. 3, 1, 4   C. 3, 2, 4   D. 4, 3, 2

Questions 32-34.

DIRECTIONS: Questions 32 through 34 are to be answered on the basis of the following infor-
              mation.
    1. Call Roger Epstein, Ashoke Naipaul, Jon Anderson, and Sarah Washington on
        April 19 at 1:00 P.M. to set up meeting with Alika D'Ornay for June 6 in New York.
    2. Call Martin Ames before noon on April 19 to confirm afternoon meeting with Bob
        Greenwood on April 20th
    3. Set up meeting room at noon for 2:30 P.M. meeting on April 19th;
    4. Ashley Stanton contact Bob Greenwood at 9:00 A.M. on April 20 and set up meet-
        ing for June 6 at 8:30 A.M.
    5. Carol Guiland contact Shelby Van Ness during afternoon of April 20 and set up
        meeting for June 6 at 10:00 A.M.
    6. Call airline and reserve tickets on June 6 for Roger Epstein trip *to* Denver on July 8
    7. Meeting at 2:30 P.M. on April 19th

32. A chronological file for all of the above information would be 32.____

    A. 2, 1, 3, 7, 5, 4, 6   B. 3, 7, 2, 1, 4, 5, 6
    C. 3, 7, 1, 2, 5, 4, 6   D. 2, 3, 1, 7, 4, 5, 6

33. A chronological file for the date of April 19th would be 33.____

    A. 2, 3, 7, 1   B. 2, 3, 1, 7
    C. 7, 1, 3, 2   D. 3, 7, 1, 2

34. Add the following information to the file, and then create a chronological file for April 20th: 34.____
    8. April 20: 3:00 P.M. meeting between Bob Greenwood and Martin Ames.

    A. 4, 5, 8   B. 4, 8, 5   C. 8, 5, 4   D. 5, 4, 8

35. The PRIMARY advantage of computer records filing over a manual system is 35.____

    A. speed of retrieval   B. accuracy
    C. cost   D. potential file loss

KEY (CORRECT ANSWERS)

1.	B		16.	B
2.	C		17.	C
3.	D		18.	D
4.	A		19.	A
5.	D		20.	D
6.	C		21.	A
7.	B		22.	B
8.	B		23.	C
9.	C		24.	D
10.	D		25.	A
11.	D		26.	B
12.	C		27.	C
13.	B		28.	D
14.	C		29.	A
15.	D		30.	B

31.	C
32.	D
33.	B
34.	A
35.	A

———

Preparing Written Material

EXAMINATION SECTION
TEST 1

DIRECTIONS: Each short paragraph below is followed by four restatements or summaries of the information contained within it. Select the one that most completely and accurately restates the information or opinion given in the paragraph. *PRINT THE LETTER OF THE CORRECT ANSWER IN THE SPACE AT THE RIGHT*

1. Australia's koalas live solely on a diet of the leaves of the eucalyptus tree, a low-protein food that requires a koala to eat about three or four pounds of leaves a day. For most mammals, these strong-smelling leaves, saturated with toxins such as phenols and the oily compound known as cineole, are among the least digestible foods on the planet. However, the koala is equipped with a digestive system that is able to handle these toxins, trapping the tiniest leaf particles for as much as eight days while the sugars, proteins, and fats are extracted.

    1.____

    A. Because eucalyptus leaves contain a large amount of toxins and oils, it takes a long time for koalas to digest them.
    B. Koalas have to eat three or four pounds of eucalyptus leaves a day, because the leaves are so poor in nutrients.
    C. Koalas have a unique digestive system that allows them to exist solely on a diet of eucalyptus leaves, which are generally toxic and inedible.
    D. The digestive system of the koala illustrates the unique evolutionary palette of the Australian continent.

2. Norway's special geopolitical position - it was the only NATO country to share a border with Russia - drove it to adopt much more cautious policies than other European countries during the Cold War. Its decision to join NATO led to strong protests from Russia, and in order to avoid provocation, Norway's foreign policy had to balance the need for ensuring defense capability with the need to keep tensions at the lowest possible level. Norway's low-tension "base policy" made clear the nation's refusal to allow foreign military forces on Norwegian territory as long as the country is not attacked or threatened with an attack.

    2.____

    A. Norway's "base policy," in spite of its shared border with Russia, is the work of a pacifist nation that should serve as a model for foreign diplomacy everywhere.
    B. When Norway joined NATO, Russia feared a ground invasion over their shared border.
    C. The "base policy" of Norway is a perfect illustration of how much of Europe during the Cold War was a powder keg ready to explode at the slightest provocation.
    D. As the only member of the NATO alliance to border on Russia, Norway was forced to adopt a more conciliatory foreign policy than other members of the alliance.

3. During the women's suffrage movement of the early twentieth century, it was typical of many psychologists and anti-suffragists to automatically associate feminism with mental illness. In 1918, H. W. Frink wrote of feminists: "A certain proportion of at least the most militant suffragists are neurotics who in some instances are compensating for masculine trends, in others, are more or less successfully sublimating sadistic and homosexual ones." In the United States, anti-suffragists, finding comfort in psychology, concluded that suffragists all bordered hysteria and, thus, their arguments could not be taken seriously.

   3._____

   A. The relationship between suffragism and feminism led many scientists to conclude that suffragists were afflicted with some kind of mental illness.

   B. During the women's suffrage movement, anti-suffragists such as H.W. Frink tended to label women who fought for voting rights as mentally ill in order to dismiss their arguments.

   C. Responses to the women's suffrage movement are indicative of the tendency to label those who challenge the status quo as "Crazy" than to confront their arguments.

   D. Most of the women who fought for suffrage during the early twentieth century were feminists who were mentally ill.

4. All of the earth's early plant life lived in the ocean, and most of these plants were concentrated in the shallow coastal waters, where the sun's energy could be easily absorbed. Because of the constant advance and retreat of tides in these regions, the plants—mostly algae—were repeatedly exposed to the atmosphere, and were forced to adapt to life out of water. It took millions of years before plant species had evolved that could survive out of the sea altogether, with stems that drew water from the ground, and a waxy covering to keep them from drying in the sun.

   4._____

   A. After spending millions of years underwater, the earth's plants finally evolved ways of surviving on land.

   B. Most algaes today, because of evolutionary advances, are able to survive for extended periods of time out of water.

   C. Despite the fact that plants began as purely underwater organisms, they have always needed the sun's energy to survive.

   D. Land plants evolved from sea plants after millions of years in response to the gradual warming of the earth's atmosphere.

5. Because of the unique convergence of mild temperatures and abundant rain (17 feet a year), British Columbia's temperate coastal rainforest is the most biologically productive ecosystem on earth. It's also an increasingly rare and vulnerable ecosystem: in its Holocene heyday, it covered only 0.2 percent of the earth's land surface. Today, logging and other development have consumed more than half this original range.

   5._____

   A. The uniquely productive ecosystem of British Columbia's coastal rainforest has always been small, and has been reduced by human activity.

   B. Despite the fact that it is the most biologically productive ecosystem on earth, the coastal rainforest of British Columbia has been largely ignored by environmental activists.

   C. The coastal rainforests of British Columbia have been nearly devastated by logging and other development.

   D. British Columbia's coastal rainforest originated during the Holocene Era, but has declined steadily ever since.

6. The Roman Empire, which ruled much of the Western world for hundreds of years, was led by an aristocratic class famous for its tendency to drink large amounts of wine. Recently, an American medical researcher theorized that this taste for wine was eventually what caused the decline and fall of the empirenot the drinking of the wine itself, but a gradual poisoning from the lead that was used to line and seal Roman wine casks. The researcher, Dr. S.C. Gilfillan, argues that this lead poisoning specifically affected members of the Empire's ruling class, because they were the Romans most likely to consume wine and other products, like preserved fruits, that were stored in lead-lined jars.

   6.____

   A. The Roman aristocracy's taste for wine and dried fruits, according to one researcher, is a cautionary tale about the consequences of overindulgence.
   B. While the Roman Empire's ruling class suffered from widespread lead poisoning, most commoners remained in good health throughout the empire.
   C. One of the most far-fetched theories about the fall of the Roman Empire concerns itself with the lead used to line the wine casks and fruit jars of the ruling class.
   D. An American medical researcher has theorized that the fall of the Roman Empire was caused by slow poisoning from the lead used to line and seal Roman wine casks and fruit jars.

7. In the second century B.C., King Hiero of Syracuse called upon the renowned scientist, Archimedes, to find a way to see if his crown was made of pure gold or a combination of metals. Archimedes came upon the solution some time later, as he was entering a tub full of hot water and noticed that the weight of his body displaced a certain amount of water. Realizing that this same principle could be used on the crown, he forgot himself with excitement, jumping out of the tub and running naked through the town, yelling "Eureka! Eureka!"

   7.____

   A. Archimedes, in making his famous discovery, unknowingly contributed the work "Eureka" to the English vocabulary.
   B. The relative purity of gold can be determined by the amount of water it displaces when submerged.
   C. Archimedes, after discovering the solution to a scientific problem while stepping into his tub, became so excited that he ran through the town naked.
   D. The word "Eureka" has become a part of the English language because of an interesting story involving the ancient scientist, Archimedes.

8. In the nineteenth century most Americans had never heard of, let alone tasted, an abalone, the marine mollusk considered to be a delicacy by many Asians, and undisturbed abalone populations thrived all along the west coast. When the California Gold Rush of the 1840s and 1850s brought thousands of Asian immigrants to America, many of these people began to harvest the dense beds of abalone that inhabited the state's intertidal zone. The Asian harvests eventually brought in annual catches of over 4 million pounds of abalone, and as a result, some county governments passed ordinances making it illegal to dive for abalone in waters less than twenty feet deep.

   8.____

   A. The Asians who immigrated to California during the Gold Rush harvested so much abalone from intertidal waters that some governments were compelled to limit abalone diving.
   B. Abalone diving was unheard of in California before the Gold Rush, when many Asians immigrated to the state and began to harvest abalone from the intertidal zone.

C. The extreme shortage of abalone in California's intertidal waters can be traced to the Asians who immigrated during the Gold Rush.

D. The abalone of California's coastal waters generally live in waters less than twenty feet deep, where they are now protected by most county governments.

9. Maria Tallchief, the daughter of a full-blood Osage Indian from Oklahoma, was America's first internationally celebrated prima ballerina, rising to stardom at a time when classical American ballet was still struggling to gain international acceptance and acclaim. Her innovative interpretations of such classics as "Swan Lake" and "The Nutcracker" helped convince critics worldwide that American ballet was a force to be reckoned with, and her glamorous beauty helped popularize ballet in America at a time when very few people took it seriously

9.____

A. As ballet grew more popular in America, Maria Tallchief became a phenomenon in Europe, helping to secure a worldwide reputation for excellence for American ballet.

B. Nobody in American took ballet seriously until the beautiful Maria Tallchief became an international star.

C. With her beauty and technical innovations, Maria Tallchief gained unprecedented critical and popular success for American ballet.

D. Before the success of Maria Tallchief, there were not many ballet dancers in the United States worth noticing.

10. Early in the Constitutional Convention of 1787, the idea of a two-tiered legislature was agreed upon by the framers of the Constitution. The final form of each of the resulting houses, however, was an issue that was debated openly, and which was finally resolved by the "great compromise" of the Constitutional Convention. While the House of Representatives was intended to be a large, politically sensitive body, the Senate was designed to be a moderating influence that would check the powers of the House.

10.____

A. The framers of the Constitution could not agree on whether the nation's legislature should be bicameral, or two-tiered, at first, but after the "great compromise," they devised a House and Senate.

B. The Constitutional Convention of 1787 ended with the "great compromise" that gave the nation its two-tiered legislature.

C. After much behind-the-scenes dealmaking, the two-tiered legislature of the United States was devised by the framers of the Constitution.

D. The framers of the Constitution, after some debate, decided on a two-tiered legislature made up of a House of Representatives and a Senate that was less susceptible to regional politics.

11. Although scientists have succeeded in creating robots able to process huge amounts of information, they are still struggling to create one whose reasoning ability matches that of a human baby. The main challenge facing these scientists is the difficulty of understanding and imitating the complex process of human perception and reasoning, which involve the ability to register and analyze even the smallest changes in the external environment, and then to act on those changes.

11.____

A. Even the most sophisticated robot is unable to imitate innate human abilities such as learning to walk, converse or perceive depth.

B. Because of their inability to process large amounts of information, robots have yet to achieve even the most fundamental level of reasoning

C. Despite considerable technological advances, scientists have as yet been unable to produce a robot that can respond intelligently to changes in its environment.

D. Because robots cannot automatically filter out all extraneous information and focus on the most important details of a given situation, they are unable to reason as well as humans.

12. Thor Heyerdahl, a Norwegian anthropologist, had long held the opinion that the Polyne-   12.____
sian inhabitants of South Pacific islands such as Samoa, Tonga, and Fiji had actually been migrants from South America. To prove that this was possible, in 1947 Heyerdahl made a crude raft out of balsa wood, which he named after an Incan sun god, *Kon-Tiki,* and sailed from the coast of Peru to the islands east of Tahiti.

A. Thor Heyerdahl's 1947 voyage on the *Kon-Tiki* proved that Polynesians probably had common ancestors in South America.

B. While Thor Heyerdahl's Kon-Tiki voyage suggested a South American origin for Polynesians, most experts today believe the great migrations were launched from somewhere near Indonesia.

C. To support the idea that Polynesians could have sailed from South America to the Pacific Islands, Thor Heyerdahl sailed the *Kon-Tiki* from Peru to Tahiti in 1947.

D. Thor Heyerdahl's famous raft, the *Kon-Tiki,* was named for an Incan sun god, and was so well-made that it made it from Peru to Tahiti.

13. During the Age of Exploration, after thousands of miles of open sea, ships entered the   13.____
bays of the Azore Islands, west of Portugal, with tattered sails, battered hulls, crewmen weakened from scurvyand cargo holds laden with the treasure they had gained on their long trading journeys. Spanish, English and Dutch warships prowled the waters around the Azores to protect this treasure, sometimes even sinking their own ships to keep it from falling into enemy hands. During these fierce battles, many ships filled with treasure were sent to the ocean floor, where they still remain, preserved by the cold saltwater and centuries of rest.

A. Although they are now sparsely populated, the Azore Islands were once a resting place for every ship returning from a long journey to the Americas.

B. Many treasure hunters and archaeologists believe the sea floor around the Azores, a group of islands west of Portugal, still harbors some of the richest sunken trea- sure in the world.

C. Economic competition between the European powers was so intense during the Age of Exploration that captains would rather sink their own ships rather than let their treasure fall into enemy hands.

D. The rich history of the Azore Islands has deposited a large amount of sunken trea- sure in their surrounding waters.

14. The Whigs, a short-lived American political party. were wary of a domineering president,   14.____
and many of them believed that the legislative branch should govern the nation. In partic- ular, Whig leader Henry Clay often attempted to bully and belittle President John Tyler into submission. Tyler's resistance to Clay's high-handed tactics strengthened the office of the presidency, and in particular gave greater credibility to all later vice presidents who happened to succeed to the office.

A. While U.S. politics was at first dominated by the legislature, President John Tyler shifted the center of power to the presidency, while laying the groundwork for the downfall of the Whig Party.

B. President John Tyler, a failure by almost any other measure, can at least be credited with contributing to the strength of the presidency.

C. Henry Clay, who believed in a strong legislature, failed to win much influence over presidents who were not from the Whig Party.

D. President John Tyler, in resisting Henry Clay's bullying tactics, strengthened the U.S. presidency and lent credibility to the authority of vice presidential successors to the presidency.

15. By far the richest city on earth, Tokyo, Japan is also one of the most overcrowded; most of its people are only able to afford living in extremely small houses and apartments. In addition to cramped housing, Tokyo's overpopulation has created a commuter problem so grim that a corps of "pushers" has been hired by the city, to stand outside crowded commuter trains and help pack people inside. Problems such as these are so severe in Tokyo that there has been serious talk in recent years of moving Japan's capital elsewhere.   15.____

A. Despite the example of Tokyo, there is no evidence to suggest that economic wealth and overpopulation are related variables.

B. Tokyo's prosperity has led to such overcrowding that the country of Japan has recently begun to consider moving its capital to another location.

C. Despite being the richest city on earth, Tokyo, Japan is seriously overcrowded.

D. The small houses and apartments of Tokyo, along with it overcrowded transit system, are a perfect example of how economic wealth does not always improve a society's quality of life.

16. One of the greatest, and least publicized, legacies of Native American culture has been the worldwide cultivation of food staples through careful farming methods. Over centuries, tribes throughout North and South America domesticated the wild plants that have come to produce over half of the vegetables the world eats today. Corn, or maize, was first cultivated in the Mexican highlands almost seven thousand years ago, from a common wild grass called teosinte, and both potatoes and tomatoes were originally domesticated by the Peruvian Incas from native plants that still grow throughout Peru and Bolivia.   16.____

A. Explorers of the Americas carried many native vegetables back to Europe, where they continued to adapt and flourish over the centuries.

B. Today's common corn is a descendant of the wild Mexican teosinte plant, and potatoes and tomatoes were originally grown by the Incas.

C. Without the agricultural knowledge and skill of early Native Americans, much of the world today would be in danger of famine.

D. Foods that are today grown and eaten almost worldwide, such as corn, tomatoes, and potatoes, were first cultivated by the natives of North and South

17. America's transportation sector-95 percent of it driven by oil-consumes two-thirds of the petroleum used in the United States. With the 400 million cars now on the world's roads expected to grow to 1 billion by the year 2020, oil-foreign or not-and other finite fossil-fuel resources will some day be conversation pieces for the nostalgic, rather than components of the nation's energy mix.   17.____

A. In the future, most motor vehicles in the United States will be powered by an alternative energy source such as hydrogen or solar power.
B. The continued growth of the oil-dependent transportation sector is outpacing the capacity of fossil-fuel energy resources.
C. Our nation's dependence on foreign oil is a serious vulnerability that can only be corrected by increased domestic production.
D. In the future, 1 billion cars across the world will be competing for oil and gasoline.

18. Althea Gibson, the first African American to win the Wimbledon Tennis Championship, began her career by riding the subway out of her neighborhood in Harlem to 143rd Street, where she played paddle tennis against anyone who dared to challenge her. Since the Wimbledon tournament was played on grass, Gibson knew she would have to prepare herself by training on a surface that returned balls as quickly as a grass court. She found the solution to this problem in the gyms of Harlem, whose wood floors allowed her to perfect the rapid volley that helped her win two Wimbledon championships.　　18._____

A. Althea Gibson's tennis skills, including her famous volley, were developed in and around the inner-city neighborhood of Harlem.
B. Althea Gibson had to leave her neighborhood to learn tennis, but to perfect her game, she had to return home to Harlem.
C. Without the wood floors in the gyms of her Harlem neighborhood, Althea Gibson probably wouldn't have developed a volley that would help her win two Wimbledon tennis championships.
D. Although Althea Gibson achieved international fame as the first African-American to win the Wimbledon Tennis Championship, the path she followed to that championship was as unorthodox as the champion herself.

19. The greenhouse effect is a naturally occurring process that aids in heating the Earth's surface and atmosphere. It results from the fact that certain atmospheric gases, such as carbon dioxide, water vapor, and methane, are able to change the energy balance of the planet by being able to absorb longwave radiation from the Earth's surface. Without the greenhouse effect, life on this planet would probably not exist, as the average temperature of the Earth would be a chilly 5 degrees, rather than the present 59 degrees.　　19._____

A. The naturally-occurring greenhouse effect, by which atmospheric air is warmed, enables life to exist on earth.
B. The greenhouse effect is a completely natural phenomenon that has nothing to do with human activity, and in fact it is beneficial to the planet's ecosystems.
C. Human contributions to the increases in the greenhouse effect threaten life on earth.
D. In order for life to exist on earth, there must be some kind of greenhouse effect.

20. The religious and scientific communities have for centuries been at odds with each other, and held opposing viewpoints concerning the origin and nature of life. Progressive thinkers from both groups, however, claim that the two communities, in their ways of seeking answers to humanity's most important questions, share a common set of goals and procedures that would benefit greatly from a cooperative effort.　　20._____

A. Scientists and theologists will probably never agree on the origin and nature of life, though some progressive thinkers are trying to change the way the two communities talk about these issues.

B. Though most scientists do not believe in God, progressive religious thinkers are continually trying to persuade them otherwise.

C. Progressive religious and scientific thinkers have identified shared goals and questions that the two communities can work together to achieve and solve.

D. Religious thinkers, who usually scorn such scientific theories as evolution, have begun to acknowledge the usefulness of science in answering important questions.

21. The administrations of Presidents Richard Nixon and Jimmy Carter oversaw an Export-Import Bank that was increasingly active in trade promotion, with expanding programs and lending authority. During this period, expenditures for program activities expanded to five times their 1969 rate, but the bank's net income dropped sharply-the low interest rates at which the bank financed its loan programs were lowering its profits.

21._____

A. During the Nixon and Carter administrations, the budget of the Export-Import Bank grew to five times its 1969 expenditures.

B. Though the Export-Import Bank was very active during the Nixon and Carter administrations, its profits were reduced by its low interest rates.

C. Both the Nixon and Carter administrations demonstrated a lack of fiscal discipline that led to a declining net income at the Export-Import Bank.

D. Presidents Nixon and Carter both favored an activist Export-Import Bank, but while Nixon emphasized the function of trade promotion, Carter was more focused on making loans.

22. The Kombai and Korawai tribes of eastern Indonesia are known as the "tree people" for their custom of living in large tree houses, built as high as 150 feet above ground to avoid attacks from their enemies. These houses are built mostly from the fronds of the sago palm, a plant that also serves to produce one of the tree people's primary food sources-the larvae, or grub, of the scarab beetle. The tree people cultivate grubs by cutting a stretch of sago forest and then, after splitting and tying the palms together, leaving the palms to rot.

22._____

A. The food-gathering methods of the Kombai and Korawai illustrate that deforestation is not a contemporary problem.

B. The Kombai and Korawai people of eastern Indonesia rely on the sago palm for both food and housing.

C. The Kombai and Korawai fears of enemy attacks have led them to build their trees high in the forest canopy.

D. Among the world's least-tamed native cultures are the Kombai and Korawai of Irian Jaya, the easternmost region of Indonesia.

23. It's no secret that corporate and federal information networks continue to deal with increasing bandwidth needs. The appetite for datawhether it's for Internet access, file delivery, or the integration of digital voice applicationsisn't likely to level off any time soon, and most information technology professionals allow that there is cause for concern. But emerging technologies for increasing raw bandwidth, accompanied by the streamlining and maturing of transfer and switching protocols, are a good bet to accommodate the hunger for bandwidth, at least into the near future.

23._____

A. There are two ways to decrease the demand for more bandwidth over computer networks: either increase the "raw" amount of bandwidth available over an infrastructure, or devise more efficient transfer and switching protocols.

B. Emerging technologies, aimed at the constantly increasing demand for bandwidth, are some day likely to result in virtually unlimited bandwidth for computer networks.

C. Man different applications contribute to the demand for bandwidth over a computer network, and so the technologies that are devised to meet this demand must be many-faceted.

D. While there is always a need for more bandwidth on large computer networks, newer technologies promise to increase the supply in the near term.

24. In the year 805, a Japanese Buddhist monk named Dengyo Daishi returned from his studies in China with some tea seeds, which he planted on a Japanese mountainside. In China, tea had long been the favorite drink of monks, because it helped them stay awake and attentive during their long periods of meditation, and Dengyo Daishi wanted to bring this practice to Japan. Over the centuries, tea-drinking would prove to be a custom that would influence nearly every aspect of Japanese culture, and Dengyo Daishi has long been considered a sort of saint among the Japanese.   24._____

A. Because of the cultural similarities between China and Japan, it was only a matter of time before the ritual of tea-drinking made its way from the mainland to the island empire.

B. Dengyo Daishi, the first person to plant tea seeds in Japan, is revered among today's Japanese.

C. The Japanese tea-drinking custom was begun in 805 by a Buddhist monk who brought tea seeds from China.

D. Without the shared cultural traditions of Buddhism, it is unlikely that tea ever would have been imported from China to Japan.

25. Aztec women held a position in society that was far more respected than that of women in most Western civilizations of the time. For example, an Aztec wife was free to divorce a man who failed to provide for their children, or who was physically abusive, and once divorced, a woman was free to remarry whomever she chose. Perhaps the unusually high regard for Aztec women is best illustrated by the traditional Aztec religious belief that a special, elevated status in the afterlife was reserved for only two types of Aztec citizens-warriors who had died defending their tribe, and women who had died during childbirth.   25._____

A. The rights and privileges of Aztec women demonstrate that they were more respected by their societies than women of many cultures of the time.

B. In the Aztec culture, women had the same rights and status as the most exalted men.

C. Though the rights of Aztec women were still generally inferior to those of men, most Aztec women were granted a high degree of independence due to their service to the community.

D. The relatively high position that Aztec women held in their society reveals the Aztec culture to be well ahead of its time.

KEY (CORRECT ANSWERS)

1.	C	11.	C
2.	D	12.	C
3.	B	13.	D
4.	A	14.	D
5.	A	15.	B
6.	D	16.	D
7.	C	17.	B
8.	A	18.	A
9.	C	19.	A
10.	D	20.	C

21.	B
22.	B
23.	D
24.	C
25.	A

PREPARING WRITTEN MATERIAL

PARAGRAPH REARRANGEMENT
COMMENTARY

The sentences which follow are in scrambled order. You are to rearrange them in proper order and indicate the letter choice containing the correct answer at the space at the right.

Each group of sentences in this section is actually a paragraph presented in scrambled order. Each sentence in the group has a place in that paragraph; no sentence is to be left out. You are to read each group of sentences and decide upon the best order in which to put the sentences so as to form as well-organized paragraph.

The questions in this section measure the ability to solve a problem when all the facts relevant to its solution are not given.

More specifically, certain positions of responsibility and authority require the employee to discover connections between events sometimes, apparently, unrelated. In order to do this, the employee will find it necessary to correctly infer that unspecified events have probably occurred or are likely to occur. This ability becomes especially important when action must be taken on incomplete information.

Accordingly, these questions require competitors to choose among several suggested alternatives, each of which presents a different sequential arrangement of the events. Competitors must choose the MOST logical of the suggested sequences.

In order to do so, they may be required to draw on general knowledge to infer missing concepts or events that are essential to sequencing the given events. Competitors should be careful to infer only what is essential to the sequence. The plausibility of the wrong alternatives will always require the inclusion of unlikely events or of additional chains of events which are NOT essential to sequencing the given events.

It's very important to remember that you are looking for the best of the four possible choices, and that the best choice of all may not even be one of the answers you're given to choose from.

There is no one right way to solve these problems. Many people have found it helpful to first write out the order of the sentences, as they would have arranged them, on their scrap paper before looking at the possible answers. If their optimum answer is there, this can save them some time. If it isn't, this method can still give insight into solving the problem. Others find it most helpful to just go through each of the possible choices, contrasting each as they go along. You should use whatever method feels comfortable, and works, for you.

While most of these types of questions are not that difficult, we've added a higher percentage of the difficult type, just to give you more practice. Usually there are only one or two questions on this section that contain such subtle distinctions that you're unable to answer confidently, and you then may find yourself stuck deciding between two possible choices, neither of which you're sure about.

Preparing Written Material

EXAMINATION SECTION
TEST 1

DIRECTIONS: The following groups of sentences need to be arranged in an order that makes sense. Select the letter preceding the sequence that represents the best sentence order. *PRINT THE LETTER OF THE CORRECT ANSWER IN THE SPACE AT THE RIGHT.*

Question 1

1.____

1. The ostrich egg shell's legendary toughness makes it an excellent substitute for certain types of dishes or dinnerware, and in parts of Africa ostrich shells are cut and decorated for use as containers for water.
2. Since prehistoric times, people have used the enormous egg of the ostrich as a part of their diet, a practice which has required much patience and hard work-to hard-boil an ostrich egg takes about four hours.
3. Opening the egg's shell, which is rock hard and nearly an inch thick, requires heavy tools, such as a saw or chisel; from inside, a baby ostrich must use a hornlike projection on its beak as a miniature pick-axe to escape from the egg.
4. The offspring of all higher-order animals originate from single egg cells that are carried by mothers, and most of these eggs are relatively small, often microscopic.
5. The egg of the African ostrich, however, weighs a massive thirty pounds, making it the largest single cell on earth, and a common object of human curiosity and wonder.

The best order is

A. 5 4 1 2 3
B. 1 4 5 3 2
C. 4 2 3 5 1
D. 4 5 2 3 1

Question 2

2.____

1. Typically only a few feet high on the open sea, individual tsunami have been known to circle the entire globe two or three times if their progress is not interrupted, but are not usually dangerous until they approach the shallow water that surrounds land masses.
2. Some of the most terrifying and damaging hazards caused by earthquakes are tsunami, which were once called "tidal waves"— a poorly chosen name, since these waves have nothing to do with tides.
3. Then a wave, slowed by the sudden drag on the lower part of its moving water column, will pile upon itself, sometimes reaching a height of over 100 feet.
4. Tsunami (Japanese for "great harbor wave") are seismic waves that are caused by earthquakes near oceanic trenches, and once triggered, can travel up to 600 miles an hour on the open ocean.
5. A land-shoaling tsunami is capable of extraordinary destruction; some tsunami have deposited large boats miles inland, washed out two-foot-thick seawalls, and scattered locomotive trains over long distances.

The best order is

A. 4 1 3 2 5
B. 1 3 4 2 5
C. 5 1 3 2 4
D. 2 4 1 3 5

3.___

Question 3

1. Soon, by the 1940's, jazz was the most popular type of music among American intellectuals and college students.
2. In the early days of jazz, it was considered "lowdown" music, or music that was played only in rough, disreputable bars and taverns.
3. However, jazz didn't take long to develop from early ragtime melodies into more complex, sophisticated forms, such as Charlie Parker's "bebop" style of jazz.
4. After charismatic band leaders such as Duke Ellington and Count Basic brought jazz to a larger audience, and jazz continued to evolve into more complicated forms, white audiences began to accept and even to enjoy the new American art form.
5. Many white Americans, who then dictated the tastes of society, were wary of music that was played almost exclusively in black clubs in the poorer sections of cities and towns.

The best order is

A. 5 4 3 2 1
B. 2 5 3 4 1
C. 4 5 3 1 2
D. 1 2 4 3 5

4.___

Question 4

1. Then, hanging in a windless place, the magnetized end of the needle would always point to the south.
2. The needle could then be balanced on the rim of a cup, or the edge of a fingernail, but this balancing act was hard to maintain, and the needle often fell off.
3. Other needles would point to the north, and it was important for any traveler finding his way with a compass to remember which kind of magnetized needle he was carrying.
4. To make some of the earliest compasses in recorded history, ancient Chinese "magicians" would rub a needle with a piece of magnetized iron called a lodestone.
5. A more effective method of keeping the needle free to swing with its magnetic pull was to attach a strand of silk to the center of the needle with a tiny piece of wax.

The best order is

A. 4 2 5 1 3
B. 4 3 5 2 1
C. 4 5 2 1 3
D. 4 1 3 5 2

Question 5

1. The now-famous first mate of the *HMS Bounty,* Fletcher Christian, founded one of the world's most peculiar civilizations in 1790.
2. The men knew they had just committed a crime for which they could be hanged, so they set sail for Pitcairn, a remote, abandoned island in the far eastern region of the Polynesian archipelago, accompanied by twelve Polynesian women and six men.
3. In a mutiny that has become legendary, Christian and the others forced Captain Bligh into a lifeboat and set him adrift off the coast of Tonga in April of 1789.
4. In early 1790, the *Bounty* landed at Pitcairn Island, where the men lived out the rest of their lives and founded an isolated community which to this day includes direct descendants of Christian and the other crewmen.
5. The *Bounty,* commanded by Captain William Bligh, was in the middle of a global voyage, and Christian and his shipmates had come to the conclusion that Bligh was a reckless madman who would lead them to their deaths unless they took the ship from him.

The best order is

A. 4 5 3 2 1
B. 1 3 5 2 4
C. 1 5 3 2 4
D. 3 1 5 4 2

Question 6

1. But once the vines had been led to make orchids, the flowers had to be carefully hand-pollinated, because unpollinated orchids usually lasted less than a day, wilting and dropping off the vine before it had even become dark.
2. The Totonac farmers discovered that looping a vine back around once it reached a five-foot height on its host tree would cause the vine to flower.
3. Though they knew how to process the fruit pods and extract vanilla's flavoring agent, the Totonacs also knew that a wild vanilla vine did not produce abundant flowers or fruit.
4. Wild vines climbed along the trunks and canopies of trees, and this constant upward growth diverted most of the vine's energy to making leaves instead of the orchid flowers that, once pollinated, would produce the flavorful pods.
5. Hundreds of years before vanilla became a prized food flavoring in Europe and the Western World, the Totonac Indians of the Mexican Gulf Coast were skilled cultivators of the vanilla vine, whose fruit they literally worshipped as a goddess.

The best order is

A. 2 3 4 1 5
B. 2 4 3 1 5
C. 5 3 4 2 1
D. 3 4 1 2 5

7._____

Question 7

1. Once airborne, the spider is at the mercy of the air currents—usually the spider takes a brief journey, traveling close to the ground, but some have been found in air samples collected as high as 10,000 feet, or been reported landing on ships far out at sea.
2. Once a young spider has hatched, it must leave the environment into which it was born as quickly as possible, in order to avoid competing with its hundreds of brothers and sisters for food.
3. The silk rises into warm air currents, and as soon as the pull feels adequate the spider lets go and drifts up into the air, suspended from the silk strand in the same way that a person might parasail.
4. To help young spiders do this, many species have adapted a practice known as "aerial dispersal," or, in common speech, "ballooning."
5. A spider that wants to leave its surroundings quickly will climb to the top of a grass stem or twig, face into the wind, and aim its back end into the air, releasing a long stream of silk from the glands near the tip of its abdomen.

The best order is

A. 5 4 2 3 1
B. 5 2 4 1 3
C. 2 5 4 3 1
D. 2 4 5 3 1

8._____

Question 8

1. For about a year, Tycho worked at a castle in Prague with a scientist named Johannes Kepler, but their association was cut short by another argument that drove Kepler out of the castle, to later develop, on his own, the theory of planetary orbits.
2. Tycho found life without a nose embarrassing, so he made a new nose for himself out of silver, which reportedly remained glued to his face for the rest of his life.
3. Tycho Brahe, the 17th-century Danish astronomer, is today more famous for his odd and arrogant personality than for any contribution he has made to our knowledge of the stars and planets.
4. Early in his career, as a student at Rostock University, Tycho got into an argument with the another student about who was the better mathematician, and the two became so angry that the argument turned into a sword fight, during which Tycho's nose was sliced off.
5. Later in his life, Tycho's arrogance may have kept him from playing a part in one of the greatest astronomical discoveries in history: the elliptical orbits of the solar system's planets.

The best order is

A. 1 4 2 3 5
B. 4 2 3 5 1
C. 4 2 1 3 5
D. 3 4 2 5 1

Question 9

9._____

1. The processionaries are so used to this routine that if a person picks up the end of a silk line and brings it back to the origin—creating a closed circle—the caterpillars may travel around and around for days, sometimes starving ar freezing, without changing course.
2. Rather than relying on sight or sound, the other caterpillars, who are lined up end-to-end behind the leader, travel to and from their nests by walking on this silk line, and each will reinforce it by laying down its own marking line as it passes over.
3. In order to insure the safety of individuals, the processionary caterpillar nests in a tree with dozens of other caterpillars, and at night, when it is safest, they all leave together in search of food.
4. The processionary caterpillar of the European continent is a perfect illustration of how much some insect species rely on instinct in their daily routines.
5. As they leave their nests, the processionaries form a single-file line behind a leader who spins and lays out a silk line to mark the chosen path.

The best order is

    A. 4 3 5 2 1
    B. 3 5 4 2 1
    C. 3 5 2 1 4
    D. 4 5 3 1 2

Question 10

10._____

1. Often, the child is also given a handcrafted walker or push cart, to provide support for its first upright explorations.
2. In traditional Indian families, a child's first steps are celebrated as a ceremonial event, rooted in ancient myth.
3. These carts are often intricately designed to resemble the chariot of Krishna, an important figure in Indian mythology.
4. The sound of these anklet bells is intended to mimic the footsteps of the legendary child Rama, who is celebrated in devotional songs throughout India.
5. When the child's parents see that the child is ready to begin walking, they will fit it with specially designed ankle bracelets, adorned with gently ringing bells.

The best order is

    A. 2 3 4 1 5
    B. 2 5 3 1 4
    C. 5 4 1 3 2
    D. 5 3 2 1 4

Question 11

1. The settlers planted Osage orange all across Middle America, and today long lines and rectangles of Osage orange trees can still be seen on the prairies, running along the former boundaries of farms that no longer exist.
2. After trying sod walls and water-filled ditches with no success, American farmers began to look for a plant that was adaptable to prairie weather, and that could be trimmed into a hedge that was "pig-tight, horse-high, and bull-strong."
3. The tree, so named because it bore a large (but inedible) fruit the size of an orange, was among the sturdiest and hardiest of American trees, and was prized among Native Americans for the strength and flexibility of bows which were made from its wood.
4. The first people to practice agriculture on the American flatlands were faced with an important problem: what would they use to fence their land in a place that was almost entirely without trees or rocks?
5. Finally, an Illinois farmer brought the settlers a tree that was native to the land between the Red and Arkansas rivers, a tree called the Osage orange.

The best order is

A. 2 1 5 3 4
B. 1 2 3 4 5
C. 4 2 5 3 1
D. 4 2 1 3 5

Question 12

1. After about ten minutes of such spirited and complicated activity, the head dancer is free to make up his or her own movements while maintaining the interest of the New Year's crowd.
2. The dancer will then perform a series of leg kicks, while at the same time operating the lion's mouth with his own hand and moving the ears and eyes by means of a string which is attached to the dancer's own mouth.
3. The most difficult role of this dance belongs to the one who controls the lion's head; this person must lead all the other "parts" of the lion through the choreographed segments of the dance.
4. The head dancer begins with a complex series of steps, alternately stepping forward with the head raised, and then retreating a few steps while lowering the head, a movement that is intended to create the impression that the lion is keeping a watchful eye for anything evil.
5. When performing a traditional Chinese New Year's lion dance, several performers must fit themselves inside a large lion costume and work together to enact different parts of the dance.

The best order is

A. 5 3 4 2 1
B. 3 4 2 5 1
C. 3 1 5 4 2
D. 4 2 3 5 1

Question 13

13._____

1. For many years the shell of the chambered nautilus was treasured in Europe for its beauty and intricacy, but collectors were unaware that they were in possession of the structure that marked a "missing link" in the evolution of marine mollusks.
2. The nautilus, however, evolved a series of enclosed chambers in its shell, and invented a new use for the structure: the shell began to serve as a buoyancy device.
3. Equipped with this new flotation device, the nautilus did not need the single, muscular foot of its predecessors, but instead developed flaps, tentacles, and a gentle form of jet propulsion that transformed it into the first mollusk able to take command of its own destiny and explore a three-dimensional world.
4. By pumping and adjusting air pressure into the chambers, the nautilus could spend the day resting on the bottom, and then rise toward the surface at night in search of food.
5. The nautilus shell looks like a large snail shell, similar to those of its ancestors, who used their shells as protective coverings while they were anchored to the sea floor.

The best order is

A. 5 2 4 1 3
B. 5 1 2 3 4
C. 1 2 5 3 4
D. 1 5 2 4 3

Question 14

14._____

1. While France and England battled for control of the region, the Acadiens prospered on the fertile farmland, which was finally secured by England in 1713.
2. Early in the 17th century, settlers from western France founded a colony called Acadie in what is now the Canadian province of Nova Scotia.
3. At this time, English officials feared the presence of spies among the Acadiens who might be loyal to their French homeland, and the Acadiens were deported to spots along the Atlantic and Caribbean shores of America.
4. The French settlers remained on this land, under English rule, for around forty years, until the beginning of the French and Indian War, another conflict between France and England.
5. As the Acadien refugees drifted toward a final home in southern Louisiana, neighbors shortened their name to "Cadien," and finally "Cajun," the name which the descendants of early Acadiens still call themselves.

The best order is

A. 1 4 2 3 5
B. 2 1 3 5 4
C. 2 1 4 3 5
D. 5 2 3 4 1

Question 15

    15.____

1. Traditional households in the Eastern and Western regions of Africa serve two meals a day-one at around noon, and the other in the evening.
2. The starch is then used in the way that Americans might use a spoon, to scoop up a portion of the main dish on the person's plate.
3. The reason for the starch's inclusion in every meal has to do with taste as well as nutrition; African food can be very spicy, and the starch is known to cool the burning effect of the main dish.
4. When serving these meals, the main dish is usually served on individual plates, and the starch is served on a communal plate, from which diners break off a piece of bread or scoop rice or fufu in their fingers.
5. The typical meals usually consist of a thick stew or soup as the main course, and an accompanying starch—either bread, rice, *or fufu, a* starchy grain paste similar in consistency to mashed potatoes.

The best order is

    A. 5 2 3 4 1
    B. 5 1 4 3 2
    C. 1 4 5 3 2
    D. 1 5 4 2 3

Question 16

    16.____

1. In the early days of the American Midwest, Indiana settlers sometimes came together to hold an event called an apple peeling, where neighboring settlers gathered at the homestead of a host family to help prepare the hosts' apple crop for cooking, canning, and making apple butter.
2. At the beginning of the event, each peeler sat down in front of a ten- or twenty-gallon stone jar and was given a crock of apples and a paring knife.
3. Once a peeler had finished with a crock, another was placed next to him; if the peeler was an unmarried man, he kept a strict count of the number of apples he had peeled, because the winner was allowed to kiss the girl of his choice.
4. The peeling usually ended by 9:30 in the evening, when the neighbors gathered in the host family's parlor for a dance social.
5. The apples were peeled, cored, and quartered, and then placed into the jar.

The best order is

    A. 1 5 3 4 2
    B. 2 5 3 4 1
    C. 1 2 5 3 4
    D. 2 1 5 4 3

Question 17   17.____

1. If your pet turtle is a land turtle and is native to temperate climates, it will stop eating some time in October, which should be your cue to prepare the turtle for hibernation.
2. The box should then be covered with a wire screen, which will protect the turtle from any rodents or predators that might want to take advantage of a motionless and helpless animal.
3. When your turtle hasn't eaten for a while and appears ready to hibernate, it should be moved to its winter quarters, most likely a cellar or garage, where the temperature should range between 40° and 45° F.
4. Instead of feeding the turtle, you should bathe it every day in warm water, to encourage the turtle to empty its intestines in preparation for its long winter sleep.
5. Here the turtle should be placed in a well-ventilated box whose bottom is covered with a moisture-absorbing layer of clay beads, and then filled three-fourths full with almost dry peat moss or wood chips, into which the turtle will burrow and sleep for several months.

The best order is

A. 1 4 3 5 2
B. 3 4 2 5 1
C. 3 2 4 1 5
D. 4 5 2 3 1

Question 18   18.____

1. Once he has reached the nest, the hunter uses two sturdy bamboo poles like huge chopsticks to pull the nest away from the mountainside, into a large basket that will be lowered to people waiting below.
2. The world's largest honeybees colonize the Nepalese mountainsides, building honeycombs as large as a person on sheer rock faces that are often hundreds of feet high.
3. In the remote mountain country of Nepal, a small band of "honey hunters" carry out a tradition so ancient that 10,000 year-old drawings of the practice have been found in the caves of Nepal.
4. To harvest the honey and beeswax from these combs, a honey hunter climbs above the nests, lowers a long bamboo-fiber ladder over the cliff, and then climbs down.
5. Throughout this dangerous practice, the hunter is stung repeatedly, and only the veterans, with skin that has been toughened over the years, are able to return from a hunt without the painful swelling caused by stings.

The best order is

A. 2 4 3 5 1
B. 2 4 1 5 3
C. 5 3 2 4 1
D. 3 2 4 1 5

Question 19

19.____

1. After the Romans left Britain, there were relentless attacks on the islands from the barbarian tribes of northern Germany—the Angles, Saxons, and Jutes.
2. As the empire weakened, Roman soldiers withdrew from Britain, leaving behind a country that continued to practice the Christian religion that had been introduced by the Romans.
3. Early Latin writings tell of a Christian warrior named Arturius (Arthur, in English) who led the British citizens to defeat these barbarian invaders, and brought an extended period of peace to the lands of Britain.
4. Long ago, the British Isles were part of the far-flung Roman Empire that extended across most of Europe and into Africa and Asia.
5. The romantic legend of King Arthur and his knights of the Round Table, one of the most popular and widespread stories of all time, appears to have some foundation in history.

The best order is

   A. 5 4 3 2 1
   B. 5 4 2 1 3
   C. 4 5 2 3 1
   D. 4 3 2 1 5

Question 20

20.____

1. The cylinder was allowed to cool until it sould stand on its own, and then it was cut from the tube and split down the side with a single straight cut.
2. Nineteenth-century glassmakers, who had not yet discovered the glazier's modern techniques for making panes of glass, had to create a method for converting their blown glass into flat sheets.
3. The bubble was then pierced at the end to make a hole that opened up while the glassmaker gently spun it, creating a cylinder of glass.
4. Turned on its side and laid on a conveyor belt, the cylinder was strengthened, or tempered, by being heated again and cooled very slowly, eventually flattening out into a single rectangular piece of glass.
5. To do this, the glassmaker dipped the end of a long tube into melted glass and blew into the other end of the tube, creating an expanding bubble of glass.

The best order is

   A. 2 5 3 4 1
   B. 2 4 5 3 1
   C. 3 5 2 4 1
   D. 3 1 4 5 2

Question 21

1. The splints are almost always hidden, but horses are occasionally born whose splinted toes project from the leg on either side, just above the hoof.
2. The second and fourth toes remained, but shrank to thin splints of bone that fused invisibly to the horse's leg bone.
3. Horses are unique among mammals, having evolved feet that each end in what is essentially a single toe, capped by a large, sturdy hoof.
4. Julius Caesar, an emperor of ancient Rome, was said to have owned one of these three-toed horses, and considered it so special that he would not permit anyone else to ride it.
5. Though the horse's earlier ancestors possessed the traditional mammalian set of five toes on each foot, the horse has retained only its third toe; its first and fifth toes disappeared completely as the horse evolved.

The best order is

A. 3 5 2 1 4
B. 5 3 2 4 1
C. 3 2 5 1 4
D. 5 2 3 1 4

Question 22

1. The new building materials—some of which are twenty feet long, and weigh nearly six tons—were transported to Pohnpei on rafts, and were brought into their present position by using hibiscus fiber ropes and leverage to move the stone columns upward along the inclined trunks of coconut palm trees.
2. The ancestors built great fires to heat the stone, and then poured cool seawater on the columns, which caused the stone to contract and split along natural fracture lines.
3. The now-abandoned enclave of Nan Madol, a group of 92 man-made islands off the shore of the Micronesian island of Pohnpei, is estimated to have been built around the year 500 A.D.
4. The islanders say their ancestors quarried stone columns from a nearby island, where large basalt columns were formed by the cooling of molten lava.
5. The structures of Nan Madol are remarkable for the sheer size of some of the stone "logs" or columns that were used to create the walls of the offshore community, and today anthropologists can only rely on the information of existing local people for clues about how Nan Madol was built.

The best order is

A. 5 4 3 2 1
B. 5 3 1 4 2
C. 3 5 4 2 1
D. 3 1 4 2 5

Question 23

1. One of the most easily manipulated substances on earth, glass can be made into ceramic tiles that are composed of over 90% air.
2. NASA's space shuttles are the first spacecraft ever designed to leave and re-enter the earth's atmosphere while remaining intact.
3. These ceramic tiles are such effective insulators that when a tile emerges from the oven in which it was fired, it can be held safely in a person's hand by the edges while its interior still glows at a temperature well over 2000° F.
4. Eventually, the engineers were led to a material that is as old as our most ancient civiliza-tionsglass.
5. Because the temperature during atmospheric re-entry is so incredibly hot, it took NASA's engineers some time to find a substance capable of protecting the shuttles.

The best order is

    A. 5 2 1 3 4
    B. 2 5 4 1 3
    C. 2 3 1 2 5
    D. 5 4 3 1 2

Question 24

1. The secret to teaching any parakeet to talk is patience, and the understanding that when a bird "talks," it is simply imitating what it hears, rather than putting ideas into words.
2. You should stay just out of sight of the bird and repeat the phrase you want it to learn, for at least fifteen minutes every morning and evening.
3. It is important to leave the bird without any words of encouragement or farewell; otherwise it might combine stray remarks or phrases, such as "Good night," with the phrase you are trying to teach it.
4. For this reason, to train your bird to imitate your words you should keep it free of any dis-tractions, especially other noises, while you are giving it "lessons."
5. After your repetition, you should quietly leave the bird alone for a while, to think over what it has just heard.

The best order is

    A. 1 4 2 5 3
    B. 1 2 4 3 5
    C. 3 2 1 5 4
    D. 3 1 5 4 2

Question 25   25.____

1. As a school approaches, fishermen from neighboring communities join their fishing boats together as a fleet, and string their gill nets together to make a huge fence that is held up by cork floats.
2. At a signal from the party leaders, or *nakura,* the family members pound the sides of the boats or beat the water with long poles, creating a sudden and deafening noise.
3. The fishermen work together to drag the trap into a half-circle that may reach 300 yards in diameter, and then the families move their boats to form the other half of the circle around the school of fish.
4. The school of fish flee from the commotion into the awaiting trap, where a final wall of net is thrown over the open end of the half-circle, securing the day's haul.
5. Indonesian people from the area around the Sulu islands live on the sea, in floating villages made of lashed-together or stilted homes, and make much of their living by fishing their home waters for migrating schools of snapper, scad, and other fish.

The best order is

A. 1 5 3 4 2
B. 1 2 4 3 5
C. 5 1 2 3 4
D. 5 1 3 2 4

———

KEY (CORRECT ANSWERS)

1.	D	11.	C
2.	D	12.	A
3.	B	13.	D
4.	A	14.	C
5.	C	15.	D
6.	C	16.	C
7.	D	17.	A
8.	D	18.	D
9.	A	19.	B
10.	B	20.	A

21.	A
22.	C
23.	B
24.	A
25.	D

———

BASIC FUNDAMENTALS OF SPORTS

CONTENTS

BASIC FUNDAMENTALS OF SPORTS

PRINCIPLES OF ATHLETICS

Athletics in the Physical Training Program

❖ Athletics deserve a prominent place in the physical training program because they contribute to the increased efficiency of the student. Because of the competitive nature of athletics and their natural appeal, the students take part in them with enthusiasm. Athletic teams formed at the intramural and higher levels are a strong unifying influence and provide one of the best means of developing esprit de corps.

❖ The athletic sports selected must be vigorous to insure good conditioning value.

❖ All the components of physical fitness cannot be developed with athletics alone. These sports are beneficial primarily in sustaining interest in the program and maintaining a level of physical fitness. Therefore, athletics are to be considered as a supplement and not a substitute for the less interesting conditioning drills.

BASKETBALL

INTRODUCTION

Basketball has enjoyed increased popularity and growth within the past few years, unequaled by any other American sport. It should be comparatively easy for an instructor to create interest in basketball among student personnel, both for conditioning and recreational purposes. Few sports have the potentialities that basketball has for developing coordination, endurance, skill, teamwork, and the will to win. It is an excellent activity for the sustaining stage. One of the objectives of a physical training program is 100 percent participation. A well-organized basketball program makes it possible to more nearly accomplish this objective than any other athletic activity.

BASIC SKILLS

Men prefer to play rather than practice so, whenever possible, a part of each instruction period should be devoted to a scrimmage game. To prevent the loss of program interest, the instructor should vary the practice routine, add new plays, organize tournaments, and devise other ways to maintain enthusiasm. He should use textbooks written by professional basketball coaches to plan and teach offensive and defensive plays.

A. **Fundamentals**
   I. Shooting baskets.
      a. One-hand set shots. Shoot from a balanced position. Keep both feet on the floor. Follow through
      b. Two-hand set shots. Shoot from a balanced position and apply equal pressure on the ball with each hand. Keep both feet on the floor. Follow through.
      c. Lay-ups. Jump high, reach high before releasing the ball. Spin the ball, using the backboard when possible.
      d. Shooting while on move. This is usually a one-handed shot. Shoot off opposite foot from the hand that releases the ball.
      e. Jump shot. Jump high, release ball with one hand at apex of height. Most common shot today.
      f. Free throws. These are one-hand and two-hand underhand throws and two-hand push shots. Put a slight back spin on the ball.

2. Ball-handling.
   a. Two-hand chest pass. Step in the direction of the pass. Use a wrist action to release the ball with a back spin.
   b. One-hand and two-hand bounce pass. Step in the direction of the pass. Bounce the ball a reasonable distance in front of the receiver, putting a back spin on the ball with a wrist action.
   c. One-hand baseball pass. Step in the direction of the pass; throw as you would throw a baseball. This is used mostly for long passes.
   d. Two-hand overhead pass. Hold the ball above the head with the arms extended. Throw with a wrist action. This pass is used mainly to get the ball to the pivot man who is close to the basket.

3. Dribbling.
   a. Changing hand with ball. Only one hand may touch the ball at one time while dribbling. The hands may be alternated.
   b. Change of pace. Changing speed and direction while dribbling.
   c. Dribbling exercise with eyes not directly on ball. Change direction; change hands; keep the head up with the eyes directed toward possible passing or shooting situations.

4. Footwork.
   a. Pivoting. Give the pivotman or center special practice in pivoting. One foot remains stationary while the opposite foot is mobile.
   b. Individual defense. Stress footwork and the position of the hands and body.
   c. Check position of feet when shooting various types of shots. Points to check: the position of balance; correct foot forward when in shooting position; the distance between each foot.

B. Small Group or Team Practice.
   1. Man-to-man defense.
      1) Switching. Each defensive man is responsible for defending against a designated man, until a screen or block forces the defensive man to change defensive responsibility.
      2) Nonswitching. Each defensive man is responsible for a designated man with the defensive man going through or behind screens and blocks.
   2. Man-to-man offense. Various types of offensive formations have been especially designed to combat man-to-man defense. Use textbooks written by professional coaches for technical knowledge.
   3. Zone defense. There are numerous variations of this type defense aimed at defending a restricted area in front of the basket. The defensive target is the ball, not the man.
   4. Zone offense. The zone offense forces the defense to adjust position, as a unit, rapidly and often. Zone offense is most effective when employing rapid movement of the ball within the defense area.
   5. Defense against fast break. Stress rebound work on the offensive backboard. Stress court balance by offensive team.
   6. Fast break offense. Move down court into scoring or offensive territory quickly.

PRACTICE DRILLS

Some practice routines are -

a.   Keep-Away. Divide unit into two groups. Designate each individual's defensive responsibility by name or number. Use half of a basketball court as the playing area. The team in possession of the ball passes it among the team members until the defense gets possession of it. Basketball rules apply. Continue with each team taking turns as it gets possession of the ball.

b.   Shooting Exercise. Divide unit into small groups. Each group has a ball. Designate the various positions on the floor where the shooting practice is to be done. Use a pre-arranged scoring method. Play numerous games, giving each group an opportunity to shoot from all positions on the floor.

c.   Dribbling Exercise. Divide unit into two or three groups. Each group has a ball. Conduct a dribbling relay. Place obstacles for dribblers to avoid and designate the path each team will follow.

d.   Defense Exercises. Use the two free throw circles and the restraining circle at center court. Place five men around the outside of each circle. One man is in the center of each ring. It is the job of the man in the center to intercept or deflect the path of the ball which is passed from man to man by the men outside of the circle. No pass may be made to an adjacent man in the circle. When the man inside the circle succeeds in intercepting, deflecting, or touching the ball, the passer takes his place.

FACILITIES AND EQUIPMENT

a. Facilities. In some sections of the country, outdoor facilities may be used, and they are easily constructed. The minimum dimensions of a court for competition are approximately 74 feet by 42 feet; maximum dimensions are 94 feet by 50 feet.

b. Equipment. A basketball is the only required equipment. For highly organized competition, however, uniforms, special shoes, and other equipment may be required.

RULES

So-called college rules or, more correctly, The National Collegiate Athletic Association rules, are used in conducting basketball in the physical training program. Each year a new paper-bound guide booklet is published and sold by the NCAA.

———

CROSS-COUNTRY AND DISTANCE RUNNING

INTRODUCTION

a. Long-distance running gives some benefits that cannot be obtained in the same degree from any other sport. It builds powerful leg muscles, increases the lung capacity, and develops endurance. For these reasons, cross-country and distance running should be included in the physical training program. These sports require only a few miles of open space that is available at school. They do require time, however, and many physical training supervisors do not find it feasible to use them as individual full-time sports. Short cross-country runs and middle-distance runs can be used to supplement other activities, particularly the team sports or the sports that develop precision or agility rather than endurance. Short cross-country runs can be scheduled once a week, gradually increasing the distance as the physical condition of the men improves; or distance running can be combined with other activities such as the conditioning exercises.

b. Cross-country and the distance runs do not enjoy equal popularity with other sports, for obvious reasons. They require great endurance, and endurance requires months of rigid training. There is a common belief that long-distance running is too strenuous, often resulting in permanent injury to the heart. While distance running may be harmful to the man who overdoes the sport, when he is not in proper physical condition, the conditioned, supervised distance runner is in no greater danger of strain than the man engaged in any other athletic activity.

LONG-DISTANCE RUNS

Any run over a mile is classed as a long-distance run. The instructor may vary the distance of the run during the season, or he may standardize it at whatever length will best suit his men or the facilities available to him. Two miles is the most popular distance. Often, the two-mile run is included as an event in track and field meets, but more frequently it is treated as a separate sport. The two-mile run may be run on any type of flat outdoor course, on a regular cinder track, or on a grass or dirt course. Because the ground is often frozen too hard for long-distance running during cold weather, the two-mile run is not recommended as a winter activity except in mild climates. The sport is too strenuous for very hot weather. The run cannot be held indoors. Constant pounding of the feet on the hard surface causes shin splints and injuries to the ankle joints.

CROSS-COUNTRY RUNS

Cross-country is a distance run held on a course laid out along roads, across fields, over hills, through woods, on any irregular ground. A flat cinder or dirt track is not a suitable surface for cross-country running. Opinions vary as to the proper length of a cross-country course. Some runs are as long as six miles. Five miles used to be accepted as standard, but recently there has been a tendency to shorten the run to four or even three miles. Only if time is available for a full-season cross-country program should the physical training instructor try to train men for a five-mile course. If time is limited, or if cross-country running is being used to supplement other activities, the three-mile course is long enough for most men.

PLACE IN THE PROGRAM

Cross-country and distance running should be used only after the men reach the sustaining stage of conditioning. They should then be scheduled occasionally to provide variety in the program. Cross-country running has the advantage of allowing mass participation. Interest can be stimulated by putting the runs on a competitive basis.

BASIC SKILLS

a. Cross-Country Running Form. Running form in cross-country races varies with the terrain and the contour of the course. On the flat, use the same form as used in a two-mile run. The body lean should be between 5 and 10 percent. A lean of more than 10 percent places too much weight and strain on the legs. A lean of less than 5 percent is retarding. In running uphill, lean forward at a greater angle and cut the length of the stride. To gain an added lift, swing the arms high and bring the knees up high on each stride. Do not slow down after reaching the crest of the hill, but resume the flat course stride as soon as the ground levels off. The runner's stride will naturally lengthen in going downhill, but he should not stretch his stride or increase his pace too much. There is less control and less balance when running downhill;

therefore, there is greater danger of turning an ankle and of falling. Keep the arms low, swinging freely, and use them as a brake and as a balance. Coming onto the flat from a downhill run, do not slow down but float or coast into a flat course pace. More energy will be used in attempting to brake the speed of descent than in maintaining the faster pace and slowing down gradually. Run on the toes or the balls of the feet, rather than on the heels. Landing on the heels throughout a five-mile course would jolt the entire body injuriously. Runners who have a tendency to strike the heel on the ground should wear a cotton or sponge rubber pad in the heels of their shoes, unless their footgear has rubber heels.

    b. Racing Tactics for Cross-Country.

        1) Teams can be pitted against each other in cross-country races. Certain members of the team may need encouragement along the way. If the team runs well-bunched for most of the course, the stronger runners can lead and encourage the weaker men. The pace should be scaled to the pace of the average runner on the team. Within a mile of the finish, however, the group should break and each man run out the race for himself.

        2) If the coach prefers his team to run on an individual basis, there are several techniques for outwitting opponents. A good runner may not take the lead but stay behind an opponent and conserve his energy for the final sprint. The opponent may tire himself out trying to maintain the lead and become so discouraged when passed by a strong sprint near the finish that he will not fight to reach the tape first. If leading an opponent, a runner may discourage him by constantly increasing the lead when he is out of sight. Opportunities for doing this frequently occur at corners of the course obscured by trees or bushes. If the leading runner sprints a short distance after rounding the corner, he may increase his lead 10 or 15 yards. After this has happened two or three times, an easily discouraged opponent may cease to be a serious contender for the race.

PRACTICE METHODS

    a. Conditioning is more essential to distance and cross-country running than to any other sport. Championship distance running depends on stamina, and stamina can be developed only through constant training. A man of only average ability can become an outstanding distance runner by steady and careful training. Hiking is the best method for getting into condition before the season opens. Long walks build up the leg muscles. During the first month of the season, training should be gradual, starting with short distances and increasing day by day. At first, the legs will become stiff, but the stiffness gradually disappears if running is practiced for a while every day. To prevent strain, it is essential to limber up thoroughly each day before running.

    b. In the mass training of a large group, leaders should be stationed at the head and the rear of the column, and they should make every effort to keep the men together. After determining the abilities of the men in cross-country running, it is advisable to divide the unit into three groups. The poorest conditioned group is started first, the best conditioned group, last. The starting time of the groups should be staggered so that all of them come in about the same time. In preliminary training, the running is similar to ordinary road work in that it begins with rather slow jogging, alternating with walking. The speed and distance of the run is gradually increased. As the condition of the men improves, occasional sprints may be introduced. At first, the distance run is from one-half to one mile. It is gradually increased to two or three miles. On completing the run, the men should be required to continue walking for three or four minutes before stopping, to permit a gradual cooling off and return to normal physiological functioning.

FACILITIES AND EQUIPMENT

a. A course three or five miles long should be measured and marked by one of the three methods specified below:

1) Directional arrows fastened to the top of a tall post and placed at every point where the course turns. Such signs should also be placed at every other point where there may be doubt as to the direction of travel.

2) A lime line placed on the ground over the entire course.

3) Flags. They should be clearly visible to the runners.
   a) A red flag indicates a left turn.
   b) A white flag indicates a right turn.
   c) A blue flag indicates the course is straight ahead.

b. There should be at least one stopwatch (preferably three) for timing the runners.

RULES

a) Team Members. A cross-country team shall consist of seven men, unless otherwise agreed. In dual meets, a maximum of twelve men may be entered, but a maximum of seven shall enter into the scoring.

b) Scoring. First place shall score 1 point, second place 2, third place 3, and so on. All men who finish the course shall be ranked and tallied in this manner. The team score shall then be determined by totaling the points scored by the first five men of each team to finish. The team scoring the least number of points shall be the winner.

Note: Although the sixth and seventh runners of a team to finish do not score points toward their team's total, it should be noted that their places, if better than those of any of the first five of an opposing team, serve to increase the team score of the opponents.

c) Cancellation of Points. If less than five (or the number determined prior to the race) finish, the places of all members of that team shall be disregarded.

d) Tie Event. In case the total points scored by two or more teams result in a tie, the event shall be called a tie.

———————

SOCCER

INTRODUCTION

a.   Soccer is one of the best athletic activities for developing endurance, agility, leg strength, and a great degree of skill in using the legs. The game is the most popular sport in Europe and is the national game of many of the Central and South American countries. In recent years, it has become popular in United States schools and colleges.

b.   A soccer ball is the only equipment needed for the game, and the men can learn to play it easily. The men do not need much skill to participate, but the amount they can develop is unlimited.

PLACE IN THE PROGRAM

Soccer should be introduced into the physical training program during the latter part of the slow improvement stage and used as a competitive activity in the sustaining stage. It is primarily a spring or fall sport. Any level field is suitable for competition. The boundaries for the soccer field are similar to the dimensions for a football field. Goal posts are essential to the game, but they are easily constructed and are usually of a temporary nature, so that they may be removed when not in use.

BASIC SKILLS

a.   Passing. Passing with the feet is the basic means of moving the ball. Short passes are easier to control and can be done more accurately than long ones. Emphasis should be continually placed on skill in passing.

b.   Dribbling. The ball is dribbled by a series of kicks with the inside or outside of the foot. Do not kick with the toe. Keep the head over the ball when kicking and propel it only a short distance at a time. Keep it close to the feet. When the ball gets very far from the feet while dribbling, an opposing player can easily take it away.

c.   Instep Kicking. The instep kick, which is the basic soccer kick, is made from the knee joint instead of from the hip as in football. The toe does not come in contact with the ball. It is pointed downward and the instep (the shoe laces) is applied to the ball with a vigorous snap from the knee. For a stationary ball, the non-kicking foot is alongside the ball at the time of the kick. For a ball rolling toward the kicker, his non-kicking foot stops short of the ball; for a ball rolling away from the kicker, his non-kicking foot stops beyond the ball. The kicker must keep his eye on the ball until it has left his foot.

d.   Inside-of-the-Foot Kicking. The ball is kicked with the inside of the foot and the leg is swung from the hip. The toe is turned outward and the sole of the boot is parallel with the ground as the foot strikes the ball. The ball should be well under the body at the time of contact. This kick is used for short passes and for dribbling.

e.   Foot Trapping. The foot trap is the method of stopping the ball by trapping it between the ground and the foot. Place the sole of the foot on top of the ball at the instant it touches the ground, but do not stamp on it. Keep the foot relaxed. This is an effective way to stop a high-flying ball.

f.   Shin Trapping. The shin trap is a method of stopping the ball with the shins. Stand just forward of the spot where the ball should strike the ground and allow it to strike the shins in flight or on the bounce. Use either one or both legs from the knee down, but do not allow the ball to strike the toe.

g.   Body Trapping. The body trap is another method of gaining control of a ball in flight. Intercept the ball with any part of the upper body except the arms and hands. Keep the body relaxed and inclined toward the ball. To keep the ball from bouncing, move backward from it as it strikes the body. This will drop the ball at the feet in position for dribbling or passing.

h.   Heading. Heading is the technique for changing the direction of the flight of a ball by butting it with the head. Tense the neck muscles and jump up to meet the ball. Butt the ball with the forehead at about the hairline to reverse its direction; use the side of the head to deflect it to the side. Always watch the ball, even during contact

OFFENSIVE AND DEFENSIVE POSITIONS

The forwards usually play on the offensive half of the field and remain in a W formation. The fullbacks usually play on the defensive half of the field. The halfbacks are the backbone of the team; they move forward on the offense and back on defense. The goal keeper almost always remains within a few feet of the goal.

DRILLS TO DEVELOP BASIC SKILLS

Several drills are recommended to develop skill in kicking, passing, and shooting. The circle formation may be used for training in any of the basic skills. The ball may be headed or trapped as it is moved around or across the circle.

ABRIDGED RULES

    a. A soccer team is composed of eleven players.

    b. The player propels the ball by kicking it with the feet or any part of the legs, by butting it with his head, and by hitting it with any portion of his body except his arms or hands.

    c. The goalkeeper is the only man allowed to use his hands on the ball, but he may only handle the ball in the goalkeeper's area. The term hands includes the whole arm from the point of the shoulder down.

    d. A goal is made by causing the ball to cross completely the section of the goal line lying between the uprights and under the cross bar.

    e. Each goal scores one point for the team scoring the goal.

    f. The penalty for a foul committed anywhere on the playing field (except by the defensive team in its penalty area) is a free kick awarded to the team that committed the foul.

    g. All opponents must be at least 10 yards from the ball when a free kick is taken.

    h. The penalty for a foul committed by the defensive team in its penalty area is a penalty kick.

    i. A penalty kick is a free kick at the goal from the spot 12 yards directly in front of the goal. The only players allowed within the penalty area at the time of the kick are the kicker and the defending goalkeeper.

    j. An official game consists of four quarters.

    k. Teams change goals at the end of every quarter.

    l. In the event of a tie, an extra quarter is played.

    m. After a ball has crossed a side line and has been declared out of play, it is put back into play by a free kick from the side line by a member of the team opposing the team that caused the ball to be out of bounds. The kick is taken from the point at which the ball crosses the side line as it goes out of bounds.

    n. When the offensive team causes the ball to go behind the opposing team's goal line, excluding the portion between the goal posts, the opposing team is awarded a goal kick - a free kick taken within the goal area that must come out of the penalty area to be in play.

    o. When the defensive team causes the ball to go behind its own goal line, excluding the portion between the goal posts, the opposing team is awarded a corner kick - a free kick taken by a member of the offensive team at the quarter circle at the corner flag-post nearest to where the ball went behind the goal line. The flag-post must not be removed.

    p. The game is started and, after a goal has been scored, is resumed by placing the ball in the center of the mid-field line. Players must be on their side of the line until the ball is kicked. The ball must be kicked forward and must move at least two feet to be legal. The first kicker may not touch the ball twice in succession at the kick-off. The opposing team must be ten yards from the ball until it moves.

SOFTBALL

INTRODUCTION

a. Softball is a game that is known in every corner of the country and has become a familiar sight in every sandlot in America. During and since World War II, it has become one of the principal physical training activities.

b. Softball is patterned after baseball, but has different advantages because it requires less equipment and is easily adapted to every age group. It requires a smaller play area; the ball is larger and softer; and the bats are lighter, making them easier to handle. Because of its popularity, a majority of our young people have a general understanding of softball and softball rules, but only a comparative few possess the skill and knowledge to obtain the maximum benefit and satisfaction from the game.

PLACE IN THE PROGRAM

a. Softball is a sustaining type of activity. It does not require continuous exertion on the part of each player; however, it is an enjoyable and occasionally strenuous game that should be included in the physical training program.

b. When a group already knows something about pitching, fielding, and batting, the instructor should give only a brief review of these fundamental skills, but place more emphasis on the rules and offensive and defensive strategy. Most of the time devoted to softball should be used for organized competition.

ORGANIZATION OF INSTRUCTION

When instruction is given on the basic skills and techniques, the students should first be shown the correct method of executing each skill. The class should then be divided into groups to practice. Ample time should be provided to familiarize each individual with the technique of playing each position as well as the basic skills necessary to play every position. When this instruction is completed, the class should be divided into teams for organized competition.

BASIC SKILLS

a. Batting. Select a bat that balances easily - hands grasp the handle at a point where the butt is neither too heavy nor too light. For a right-handed batter, the left foot points at about a 45° angle toward the pitcher, and the right foot points toward homeplate. The feet are about 8 inches apart. The head and eyes face the pitcher, and the bat is over the right shoulder, hands away from the body. The batting position is slightly to the rear of the center of the plate. In swinging, keep the eyes on the ball, twisting at the waist. As a result of the twist, the arms will swing automatically. The power of the swing is developed with a snap of the wrists and the extension of the arms in the follow-through.

b. Bunting. The stance for bunting is the same as for batting. When the ball leaves the pitcher's hand, immediately bring the bat from over the shoulder, moving the right hand slightly up the handle, until the bat is directly over the plate. Rotate the body so that it faces the pitcher. The feet are comfortably apart. Meet the ball squarely, absorbing the shock with the arms. Hold the edge of the bat perpendicular to the direction in which the ball is to be bunted.

c. Base Running. Upon hitting the ball, the runner must start quickly without watching where the ball goes. He should get to the first base as fast as possible and be ready to continue running at the coach's direction. Speed is the most important factor, but running the shortest distance between bases is also essential.

d. Sliding. Use the hook slide going into the base, with the body relaxed, extending either foot in a sweeping motion, touching the toe to the bag.

e. Catching. Assume the knee bend position, with the upper arms parallel to the ground, forearms vertical, and palms down. As the ball strikes the mitt, grasp it with the bare hand. On high pitches, cup the fingers of the bare hand to prevent injury. On low pitches, extend the palms toward the pitcher with the thumbs down. Always avoid pointing the fingers toward the pitcher. The catcher must not sacrifice accuracy for speed in throwing to bases and must learn through experience when he can throw a player out at base.

f. Pitching. Pitching, to a large degree, determines a team's defensive strength, and pitching can only be developed through practice. To hold the ball, grasp it loosely with the fingers, the index, middle, and third fingers on one side and the thumb and fourth finger on the other side. The most effective manner of pitching is the windmill pitch. To start the wind-up, face the homeplate with both feet on the rubber. The ball is held in front with both hands. Raise the left foot to the rear as the right arm swings backward. The body pivots to the right, the left hand is extended and balances the motion, and the head and eyes remain on the catcher's glove. When the right arm reaches the nine o'clock position, step forward with the left foot directly toward homeplate, swing the arm forward, and twist the body to the left. With a snap of the wrist on the underhand swing, release the ball and follow through. Control is very important and must be gained through practice.

g. Infield Playing. An infielder must anticipate at all times what he should do in case he has to play the ball. On batted ground balls, he should play the ball to his front. Field each ground ball with the feet apart, hands well out in front. When the ball strikes the glove, secure it with the bare hand. The hands and arms should relax, and the arms should be drawn backward toward the right hip preparatory to the throw.

h. Outfield Playing. An outfielder should be alert and fast and able to judge the ball so he can get in the best position to catch it. It takes practice to become a successful fielder. To catch a fly ball, he extends the arms forward, forming a cup with the hands. He keeps his eyes on the ball until he has firm possession of it. He catches ground balls in the same way as the infielder (see g. above).

DRILLS

a. Pitching and Catching. Divide the class into two lines fifty feet apart; one side will pitch, the other will catch. Make corrections on form for both pitching and catching. Emphasize form and control. Change over.

b. Infield Play. Divide the class into seven-man groups. Place each group in a separate area, simulating (if necessary) the softball diamond. Designate a first, second, and third baseman, and a shortstop. Choose one man to hit balls and one to catch at homeplate. The player who hits balls first calls a play such as first base, double play, throw it home, etc. He then hits a ground ball to one of the infielders who, in turn, carries out the prescribed play. Demand enthusiasm and hustle. Change over occasionally and allow each man to play each position.

c. Outfield Play. Place seven men in the outfield, but do not designate definite positions. Have a player hit both fly and ground balls to the field. Use one player to catch balls at homeplate. After each ball has been played, have it relayed back to the hitter. Change positions so that each player has an opportunity to play in the outfield.

d. Base Running. Divide the class into fifteen-man groups. Time each runner in a complete circuit of bases. Stimulate competition. Critique each runner.

e. Hitting and Bunting. Divide the class into regular nine-man teams. Place one team in the field to shag balls. The players on the other team take turns at bat, hitting ten balls each. On the last pitch, they lay down a bunt and run to first base, trying to beat the throw. Change over.

OFFENSIVE AND DEFENSIVE STRATEGY

a. Offensive. Hit only good balls (balls in the strike zone). Runners should run out fly balls at top speed, in case the ball is dropped or an error is committed. There is a better possibility of stealing a base than of the next batter hitting safely. Do not hesitate in stealing. Do not attempt to steal third base when two men are out, because a runner should be able to score from second base on a hit or on an error. It is best to attempt to steal second base with two outs. With no outs and runners on first and second base, a bunt combined with a double steal is good strategy. A runner can usually score from third base on a fly ball or on an error.

b. Defensive. A player should always back up another player receiving a throw at a base, or a player attempting to make a play on a fly or ground ball. The player who is nearest the ball should call for it and make the catch or play. Each player should be aware of the situation and know exactly what to do if he receives the ball. Receive bunts, flys, and ground balls with both hands. Have firm possession of the ball before attempting a throw. On force plays, do not stand on the base. It is better to make certain of one out, rather than risk an error in trying for a double play. When a shorter throw can put a runner out at base, it is best to attempt the shorter throw. With runners on first and second base, it is better to force out at third than to try a double play from second to first base. An outfielder should throw the ball directly to the spot where the play is likely to be made, unless it is a long fly and a relay appears to be quicker.

SPEEDBALL

INTRODUCTION AND GENERAL DESCRIPTION

Speedball is a game that offers vigorous and varied action with plenty of scoring opportunities. It is easy to learn and provides spontaneous fun. Little equipment is needed - a ball is all that is absolutely necessary. Speedball combines the kicking, trapping, and intercepting elements of soccer; the passing game of basketball; and the punting, drop-kicking, and scoring pass of football. Two teams of eleven men each play the game under official rules, but any number of players may successfully constitute a team. An inflated leather ball, usually a soccer ball, is used. The playing field is a football field with a football goal post at each end. The game starts with a soccer-type kickoff. The kicking team tries to retain possession of the ball and advance it toward the opposite goal by passing or kicking it. Running with the ball is not allowed, so there is no tackling or interference. When the ball touches the ground, it cannot be picked up with the hands or caught on the bounce, but must be played as in soccer until it is raised into the air directly from a kick; then the hands are again eligible for use. When the ball goes out of bounds over the side lines, it is given to a player of the team opposite that forcing the ball out, and is put into play with a basketball throw-in; when it goes over the end line without a score, it is given to a player of the opposing team who may either pass or kick it onto the field. When two opposing players are contesting the possession of a held ball, the official tosses the ball up between them as in basketball. Points are scored by kicking the ball under the crossbar of the goal posts, drop-kicking the ball over the crossbar, completing a forward pass into the end zone for a touchdown, or by kicking the ball under the crossbar of the goal posts on a penalty kick.

PLACE IN THE PROGRAM

Speedball, like soccer, should be introduced into the physical training program during the latter part of the toughening stage and used as a competitive activity in the sustaining stage. It may be played any time the weather permits, but it is primarily a spring or fall activity.

BASIC SKILLS

a. Soccer Techniques.
  i. Kicking.
  ii. Passing.
  iii. Heading.
  iv. Trapping.
b. Football Techniques.
  i. Punting.
  ii. Drop-kicking.
  iii. Forward passing.
c. Basketball Techniques.
  i. Passing.
  ii. Receiving.
  iii. Pivoting.
d. Kickups and Lifts. The kickup is a play in which a player lifts the ball into the air with his feet so that he may legally play the ball with his hands. The kickup is generally used to make the transition from ground play to aerial play. The technique of making the play depends upon whether the ball is rolling or stationary. To kick up a ball rolling or bouncing toward the player, the foot is held on the ground with the toe drawn down until the ball rolls onto the foot, then the foot is raised, projecting the ball upward. If the ball is stationary, the player rolls it backward with one foot, then places the foot where the ball will roll onto it. He can then lift the ball with that foot. If a ball is rolling away from the player, he should stop it with a foot and play it as a stationary ball. There is also a method of raising the ball by standing over it with a foot on either side. He presses his feet against the ball and jumps into the air, propelling the ball into his hands.

OFFENSIVE POSITIONS AND STRATEGY

The positions of the players in speedball are much the same as in soccer. However, some of the positions are designated by different names. There are eleven players on each team. The forward line is composed of five players: the right end, right forward, center, left forward, and left end. The second line consists of right halfback, fullback, and left halfback. In the next line is the right guard and left guard. The player who defends the_ goal is the goal guard. The strategy employed in speedball during offensive play is very similar to that of soccer.

DEFENSIVE PLAY

There are two types of defensive formations in speedball: man-for-man and position defense. Man-for-man defense is recommended for beginning players.

ABRIDGED RULES

a. The Field. 360 feet long and 160 feet wide (a regulation football field).

b. Players. Eleven on a team. The goal guard has no special privileges.

c. Time. Ten-minute quarters, two minutes between. Ten minutes between halves. Five minutes for extra overtime periods. (Begin first overtime by a jump ball (see g(3) below) at center, same goals; change goals in the event of a second overtime period.)

d. Winner of Toss. The winner of the toss has the choice of kicking, receiving, or defending a specific goal.

e. Starting Second and Fourth Quarters. The ball is given to the team that had possession at the end of the previous quarter, out of bounds, as in basketball.

f. Half. The team that received at the start of the first half kicks off at the beginning of the second half.

g. The Game. The game is started with a kickoff from the middle line (50-yard line), both teams being required to remain back of their respective restraining lines until the ball is kicked. The ball must travel forward.

1. The most characteristic feature of the playing rules of speedball is the differentiation between a fly ball (or aerial ball) and a ground ball. A player is not permitted to touch a ground ball with his hands and must play it as in soccer. A fly ball is one that has risen into the air directly from the foot of a player (example: punt, drop-kick, place-kick, or kickup). Such a ball may be caught with the hands provided the catch is made before the ball strikes the ground again. A kickup is a ball that is so kicked by a player that he can catch it himself. A bounce from the ground may not be touched with the hand because it has touched the ground since being kicked. This rule prohibits the ordinary basketball dribble, but one overhead dribble (throwing the ball into the air and advancing to catch it before it hits the ground) is permitted.

2. If a team causes the ball to go out of bounds over the side lines, a free throw-in (any style) is given to the opposing team. When the ball goes over the end line without scoring, it is given to the opponents who may pass or kick from out of bounds at that point.

3. In case two players are contesting the possession of a held ball, even in the end zone, a tie ball is declared and the ball is tossed up between them.

4. The kick-off is made from any place on or behind the 50-yard line. Team A (the kicking team) must be behind the ball when it is kicked. Team B must stay back of its restraining line (ten yards' distance) until the ball is kicked (penalty - a violation). The ball must go forward before A may play it (penalty - violation). Kick off out of bounds to opponents at that spot. A kick-off touched by B and going out of bounds, no impetus added, still belongs to B. A kick-off, in possession and control of B and then fumbled out of bounds, belongs to A at that spot. A field goal from kick-off (under crossbar, etc.) scores 3 points.

h. Scoring Methods.
   1. Field goal (3 points). A soccer-type kick, in which a ground ball is kicked under the crossbar and between the goal posts from the field of play or end zone. (A punt going straight through is not a field goal for it is not a ground ball. The ball must hit the ground first.) A drop-kick from the field of play that goes under a crossbar does not count as a field goal. A drop-kick from the end zone that goes under the crossbar counts as a field goal; if it goes over the crossbar, it is ruled as a touch back.
   2. Drop-kick (2 points). A scoring drop-kick must be made from the field of play and go over the crossbar and between the uprights. The ball must hit the ground before it is kicked (usually with the instep).
   3. End goal (1 point). This is a ground ball which receives its impetus (kicked or legally propelled by the body) from any player, offensive or defensive, in the end zone and passes over the end line but not between the goal posts.
   4. Penalty kick (1 point). This is a ball kicked from the penalty mark that goes between the goal posts and under the crossbar. The penalty mark is placed directly in front of the goal at the center of the goal line.
   5. Touchdown (1 point). A touchdown is a forward pass from the field of play completed in the end zone. The player must be entirely in the end zone. If he is on the goal line or has one foot in the field of play and the other in the end zone, the ball is declared out of bounds. If a forward pass is missed, the ball continues in play but must be returned to the field of play before another forward pass or drop-kick may be made.
i. Substitutions. Substitutions may be made any time when the ball is not in play. If a player is withdrawn, he may not return during that same period.
j. Time Out. Three legal time-outs of two minutes each are permitted each team during the game.
k. Fouls.
   1. Personal (four disqualify). Kicking, tripping, charging, pushing, holding, blocking, or unnecessary roughness of any kind, such as running into an opponent from behind. Kicking at a fly ball and thereby kicking an opponent.
   2. Technical. Illegal substitution, more than three time-outs in a game, unsportsmanlike conduct, unnecessarily delaying the game.
   3. Violation. Traveling with the ball, touching a ground ball with the hands or arms, double overhead dribble, violating tie ball, and kicking or kneeing a fly ball before catching it.
   4. Penalties. (The offended player shall attempt the kick.)

	Penalty	Location
Personal	In field of play	1 kick with no follow-up
Technical	In field of play	1 kick with no follow-up
Violation	In field of play	Out of bound to opponent
Personal	In end zone	2 kick with no follow-up on last kick
Technical	In end zone	1 kick with no follow-up
Violation	In end zone	1 kick with no follow-up

l. Summary of Fouls.
   1. Fouls in the field of play allow no follow-up while fouls in the end zone always allow follow-up.
   2. On penalty kicks, with no follow-up, only the kicker and goalie are involved.
   3. On penalty kicks, with a follow-up, the kicking side is behind the ball and the defending side behind the end line or in the field of play. No one is allowed in the end zone or between the goal posts except the goal guard. The kicker cannot play the ball again until after another player plays it, and he must make an actual attempt at goal.

———

TOUCH FOOTBALL

INTRODUCTION

Touch football has become a major active game on the lower levels of competition. Considering its similarity to football and yet its comparative simplicity, it is easy to understand the popularity of the game. The modification of regulation football rules for touch football eliminates the necessity for much special equipment, training, and professional leadership. Touch football encourages participation, reduces the number of injuries, and simplifies the teaching of fundamental rules, techniques, and skills.

PLACE IN THE PROGRAM

Touch football is an excellent conditioning activity, and it should be included in both the physical training and intramural programs. It may be used in the latter part of the toughening stage and during the sustaining stage of physical conditioning. It should be played in the fall when the interest in football is at its peak. Any level field can be used. Goal posts are desirable but not absolutely necessary.

ORGANIZATION OF INSTRUCTION

Most men know something about football, but not all have had an opportunity to play. Several short periods should be devoted to the instruction of all men in the basic fundamentals. A desirable method is to give five to ten minutes of instruction at the beginning of each football period and follow it by actual play.

BASIC SKILLS

a. Offensive Stance. Touch football emphasizes speed; therefore, a high offensive stance should be used to facilitate a fast getaway. The feet should be about shoulder width apart and parallel, knees bent, thighs just above the horizontal and back nearly parallel with the ground. The head and eyes are up, and the right hand is extended straight downward, the fingers curled under, the thumb toward the rear. The left arm rests on the left thigh. There are many variations of this basic stance that may be used. The general principles are: Keep the feet spread for balance, the body under control, and the head up with the eyes on an opponent or the ball.

b. Defensive Stance. This type stance may be similar to the offensive stance or somewhat higher to allow for better visibility and free use of the hands to ward off blockers. The same principles of balance, body control, and vision used in the offensive stance are applicable to the defensive stance.

c. Blocking. Touch football rules do not permit the blocker to have both feet off the ground at the same time (flying block); therefore, the blocker should maintain a wide base for shoulder, upright, or cross-body blocks. For the shoulder block, the hands should be close to the chest, the elbows raised sideward, the feet under the body and widely spread, the head up, and the buttocks low. Upon contact, the feet should be moved rapidly in short, choppy steps to force the body forward, thus keeping the shoulder in contact with the opponent. The upright block is useful in the open field and is executed by the player while standing nearly erect. The feet are widely spread, knees slightly bent, the trunk inclined slightly forward, and the head erect. The arms are raised, and the hands are placed on the chest, forearms forward to contact the opponent. Due to the nature of the block, the opponent is contacted above the waist. In performing the cross-body block, the blocker uses the hip to contact the opponent, usually in the area of the thighs. The execution of this type of block requires the blocker to throw his head, shoulders, and arms past the target area, thus bringing his hip into contact with his opponent. Then, assisted by movement of the hands and feet which are in contact with the ground, he forces the opponent backward or down. The shoulder, upright, or cross-body blocks may be used in the line or in the open field.

d. Ball Carrying. The first point to stress in ball carrying is the grip of the ball. The ball is placed in the arm with its long axis parallel to the forearm. It is held firmly and close to the body. The hand grips the lower point of the ball with the fingers spread to form a firm grip. It is difficult to teach the fine points of ball carrying in a few hours of instruction. Stress the principles. Teach runners to carry the ball in the arm away from the opponent. The runner should be cautioned to follow his interference and to keep his head up so he can avoid his opponents.

e. Forward Passing. Forward passing is one of the principal means of advancing the ball in touch football. Teach the method of gripping or holding the ball with the fingers spread on the laces and toward the end of the ball, cocking the arm with the hand holding the ball close to the head and the wrist rotated so that the rear point of the ball is pointing toward the head. The ball is delivered with a baseball catcher's peg motion, by extending the arm and imparting a spiral to the ball. To make a successful forward pass, it is usually best for the passer to have the feet spread comfortably and in contact with the ground, the free hand extended to aid the balance. He throws the ball to a spot where the receiver can catch it without breaking his stride. Do not allow beginners to attempt jump passes, as the successful throwing of this type of pass requires the skill of an experienced forward passer.

f. Pass Receiving. To catch a forward pass requires the receiver to keep his eyes on the ball, to run to the spot where he can reach the ball, to catch it without breaking stride, and to take it out of the air by relaxing the hands as the ball strikes. In receiving a pass over the shoulder, the little fingers are facing, with the thumbs outward and all fingers spread. In catching a pass while facing the passer, the receiver should catch a high pass with the thumbs facing and the little fingers out; and a low pass with the little fingers facing and the thumbs pointing outward.

DRILLS TO DEVELOP FUNDAMENTALS

It is recommended that the time available for instruction in the fundamentals be used in teaching the following skills: stance, shoulder block, cross-body block, forward passing, and pass receiving.

a. Stance Drill. Use the extended rectangular formation. Demonstrate the stance and tell the men they will execute the drill by the numbers. At the count of one, place the feet in position. At the count of two, bend the knees and trunk. At the count of three, lean forward and place one hand on the ground. After checking for errors and making corrections, command "UP" and execute the drill again. Have the men do this several times before progressing to the next drill.

b. Blocking Drills. All the blocks may be practiced by forming the class into two lines facing one another and having the men pair off. Explain the drill, demonstrate the block desired, and designate one line as blockers and the other as opponents. After several practice blocks, have the blockers become the opponents and the opponents become the blockers. During the course of the drill, emphasize the three phases of blocking: the approach, contact, and follow-through.

c. Forward Passing Drill. Form the class in groups of ten men each. The groups form two lines with the men about ten feet apart and the two lines ten to fifteen yards apart. Using at least one ball to a group, practice grip, balance, throwing with a spiral, and follow-through. The ball is thrown by each man, in turn, to the next man in the opposite line who catches it and throws.

d. Passing and Receiving Drill. Each of the groups is formed as for the drill outlined in c. above. One man, the center, is stationed between the two files with the ball. One file is designated as passers and the other as receivers. The center snaps the ball to the first passer. He passes to the first receiver who runs down the field at the snap of the ball. The receiver catches the pass and returns the ball to the center. Upon his return, the receiver joins the "passer" file and the passer joins the "receiver" file. This rotation continues until all men have an opportunity to throw and receive forward passes.

e. Other Drills. If time permits, other fundamental drills may be included, such as snapping the ball from center, kicking, lateral passing, and other individual skills of a specialty nature.

OFFENSIVE FORMATIONS AND PLAY

a. A nine-man team is recommended. Three offensive formations are suggested for this size team. Of the three formations suggested, the double wing-back is the best.

b. To complete the instruction in offensive play, it will be necessary to insure that some member of the team can perform the individual specialties. These special skills are passing the ball from center, punting, free kicking for kick-offs, backfield pivots, handoffs, etc.

c. Men like to develop their own plays and should be encouraged to do so. Time must be made available for them to practice such plays before using them in a game.

DEFENSIVE PLAY

The class should be shown several defensive formations. Four different ones are applicable for the nine-man team. The selection of a defense depends upon the opponent's offense. The 4-2-2-1 and the 5-1-2-1 are better pass defense formations than the 4-3-2 and the 5-2-2. The latter formations are weak "down the middle". However, the 4-3-2 and 5-2-2 are stronger against a running attack. If fewer men are employed on a team, the defense could be altered by eliminating either linemen or backs, as required.

ORGANIZATION AND ADMINISTRATION

a. The instructor may divide the class into teams from the roster or by selecting team captains who, in turn, choose the remaining members of their teams.

b. The officials may be assistant instructors or selected individuals from the class. It is suggested that there should be at least one official for each game that is played. Close supervision of play and strict enforcement of rules are necessary to prevent injuries from excessive roughness.

c. To insure the success of touch football in a physical training period, the teams should be organized into a class league to stimulate interest and competition, and to select the championship team.

d. There should be one ball for each fifteen men.

e. The area for practice and play should be grassed and level. The field should conform as nearly as possible to the size specified in paragraph 9a(1).

RULES

It is important that the participants know the rules that govern touch football. It increases the players' enjoyment in the activity, lessens the chance of injury, and results in an organized contest. Official National Collegiate Athletic Association football rules shall govern all play except those special rules pertinent to touch football, as stated in the following subparagraphs.

    a. Rule I - Field and Equipment.

        1. Section 1 - Field. The game shall be played on a regulation football field with goal posts. When space is limited, the dimensions of the field may be reduced to 300 feet long by 120 feet wide.

        2. Section 2 - Uniforms. Distinctive jerseys, shorts, sweat suits, or trousers, and basketball shoes or regulation footwear may be worn. Pads, helmets, and cleated shoes are not authorized.

    b. Rule II - Length of Game.

        1. Section 1 - Periods. The game shall be played in four periods each ten minutes in length, with a one-minute interval between the first and second and the third and fourth periods; and with a ten-minute interval between the second and third periods.

        2. Section 2 - Contest. By mutual agreement of opposing coaches or captains, before the start of contest, the length of the periods may be shortened or lengthened.

        3. Section 3 - Time Out. Time out shall be taken -

            a. After a touchdown, field goal, safety, or touch back.

            b. During a try for a point.

            c. After an incomplete forward pass.

            d. When the ball goes out of bounds.

            e. During the enforcement or declination of penalties.

    c. Rule III - Players and Substitutes.

        1. Section 1 - Players (nine-man game). Each team shall consist of nine players. The offensive team shall have a minimum of five players on the scrimmage line when the ball is snapped. Note: The following diagram designates the position of the players -

END   GUARD   CENTER   GUARD   END

QUARTERBACK

HALFBACK HALFBACK

FULLBACK

2. Section 2 - Players (six-man game). Each team shall consist of six players. The offensive team shall have a minimum of three players on the scrimmage line when the ball is snapped.
   Note: The following diagram designates the position of the players -

END   CENTER   END

HALFBACK   HALFBACK

FULLBACK

3. Section 3 - Substitutions. Unrestricted substitutions may be made when
   a. The ball is dead.
   b. The clock is running, provided substitutions are completed and the ball is snapped within 25 seconds after the ball is ready for play.

d. Rule IV - Playing Regulations.
   1. Section 1 - Starting the game and putting ball in play after any score shall be as prescribed by the NCAA Football Rule Book, with exception of Rule 4, Sections 2 and 3.
   2. Section 2 - Kick-off. The receiving team, in a nine-man game, shall have three players within five yards of its own restraining line until the ball is kicked.
   3. Section 3 - Restriction. In a six-man game, the only restriction on the receiving team is that all players must remain back of their own restraining line until the ball is kicked.
   4. Section 4 - Fumbled Ball. A ball that is fumbled and touches the ground during a run, kick, or lateral pass play, may not be advanced by either team. The ball may be touched and recovered by any player. It shall be dead and in possession of the player who first touches it after it strikes the ground.
      Note: Players shall be warned against diving on fumbled balls and may be penalized for unnecessary roughness.
   5. Section 5 - Fumbled ball or lateral pass. A fumbled ball or lateral pass, intercepted or recovered before it touches the ground, may be advanced by any player.
   6. Section 6 - Downed ball by legal touch. The player in possession of the ball is downed and the ball is dead when such player is touched by an opponent with both hands simultaneously above the waist and below the head.
   7. Section 7 - Forward passing. One forward pass may be made during each scrimmage play from behind the passer's scrimmage line.
   8. Section 8 - Eligible receivers. All players of offensive and defensive teams are eligible to receive forward passes. Two or more receivers may successively touch a forward pass.

e. Rule V - Fouls and Penalties. Section 1 - Use of hands and arms. For both offense and defense, as prescribed in NCAA Football Rule Book.

VOLLEYBALL

INTRODUCTION

a. Volleyball is a popular sport. The game entails much physical activity, yet it is not strenuous. It is, therefore, a game for young and older men alike, for beginners and for skilled players. It may be played indoors or outdoors on any type of terrain. As an informal activity, volleyball can be played by any number of men; as an organized activity, it provides, as few other sports do, a game for twelve men to play in a limited area.

b. While volleyball requires no great skill to play, it does permit a high degree of proficiency. A man naturally gets more enjoyment when he knows the game and plays it well. For this reason, instruction in the basic skills should be provided.

ORGANIZATION

Usually a ten to fifteen-minute period of instruction, followed by scrimmage during the first three or four classes is enough to teach the basic skills, rules, and techniques of volleyball. More time can be given to teaching basic skills, if available, but the emphasis is on competitive play rather than on formal instruction. It is best to lecture and demonstrate to the entire class, then divide the class into smaller groups for practice. For drills and scrimmages, divide the class so that there will be from twelve to twenty-four men to each court. One court may be used for instruction by allowing twelve players at a time to execute the drill while the other class members observe, act as coaches, or retrieve balls. After the instruction phase of training has been completed, divide the class into six-man teams. Organize the teams on the basis of ability. All teams should be as nearly equal as possible.

PLACE IN THE PROGRAM

Volleyball may be used occasionally as a competitive activity during the sustaining stage. It is a year-round sport, but it should be included in the physical training program only when it is impractical to conduct a more strenuous activity. It is an excellent self-interest activity.

BASIC SKILLS

a. Passing.

    1. Handling the low ball. A ball that is lower than the waist is one of the easiest to hit, but is also a frequent cause of the fouls of holding or carrying the ball. The best position for handling a low ball is to have the feet staggered, knees flexed, and arms flexed at the elbows and rotated so the thumbs are pointing outward, the palms up. When the fingers contact the ball, the entire body reacts in a lifting motion. The arms and hands swing upward in a scooping action. It is important that the fingers, not the palms, contact the ball, and that the ball is batted, not thrown.

    2. Handling the high ball. The chest pass is the most effective method of playing the ball. To receive the ball, the feet are staggered, knees are flexed, and the body is tilted forward. The elbows are raised sideward to a point in line with the shoulders. The wrists are extended in line with the forearm and the arms, wrists, and hands are rotated inward. To pass the ball, the hands are chest high, thumbs pointing inward. The fingers are flexed, forming a cup, allowing them to contact the ball. On contact with the ball, the wrists are snapped while the fingers and elbows are pushed upward, sending the ball upward. A high ball is much easier to handle than a low one.

b. Serving.

    1. The underhand serve. Take a position behind the back line facing the net, left foot forward, holding the ball in the palm of the left hand. The left knee is flexed, the right knee is straight. Swing the right arm back and at the same time move the left hand (holding the ball) across the body in line with the right hip. Then swing the right arm forward hitting the ball off of the left hand with the palm of the right hand, raising the hips and arching the back in the same motion. Be certain to swing the right arm in a straight line, or the ball will be difficult to control.

2. Placement of the serve. When the opposition is in formation, the server should try to place the ball in the right or left back area, and not near the net.

c. Setting up. A setup is a ball hit into the air near the net by one player, so a teammate may hit or "spike" it sharply downward into the opponent's court. The chest pass is the best pass to use. The ball is sent approximately ten feet into the air toward the spiker so it will descend from four to twenty inches from the net.

d. Spiking. The spike is a leap into the air and a sharp downward hitting of the ball into the opponent's court. A spiker must be able to spring easily from the floor, judge the movement of the ball, and strike it with a downward movement of his arm. To jump from the floor, step off with one foot and jump with the other. Stand with the right or left side to the net, facing the setup man. Much depends upon the setup man to place the ball in the proper position. The spiker jumps into the air and strikes the ball above its center so as to drive it downward. A snapping movement of the arm and wrist will drive the ball forward and downward with power and control. Aim for a weak spot in the opponent's defense.

e. Blocking. The block is a technique of defense used to prevent a spiker from driving the ball across the net. It is an attempt by one or more defensive players at the net to block a hard hit shot by using the force of the ball to send it immediately back into the opponent's court. An effective block is for forwards on the defensive team to spring into the air at the time of the spike, placing both hands and arms in the expected path of the ball. An effective block tends to upset the offense and presents another element for the spiker to worry about. To be effective, the blocker must anticipate the path of the ball and time his block with the spike.

DRILLS TO DEVELOP BASIC SKILLS
a. Passing.
1. Divide the class into twenty-four-man groups. Have them form a circle and begin passing a ball around the circle trying to prevent it from touching the floor.
2. Divide each group with twelve men on a side facing the net. Form four ranks per side, with the first ranks passing the ball back and forth over the net until a pass is incomplete. Then have the second rank move up. Place the groups in a regular playing formation concentrating only on passing, using both the chest pass and the low pass.
b. Serving. Break the men into two groups - one line to act as servers, the other as retrievers. Change over frequently giving each man a chance. When the men can control the serve, have each server try to place the ball in the various areas of the court.
c. Spiking. Have two files on one side of the court facing the net. One file is the spiking file, the other is the setup line. One man from each file moves up to the net at one time. The spiker tosses to the setup, the setup sets the ball up for spiker, and the spiker drives it over the net. Rotate the files.

OFFENSIVE PLAY
a. Each member of a good offensive team should -
1. Be able to serve.
2. Know the capabilities and weaknesses of each of his teammates.
3. Have an understanding of all offensive plays.
4. Be able to analyze the opponent's weaknesses.
5. Always know what area of the court he is responsible for.
6. Be ready to "back up" a teammate receiving the ball.
b. The big offensive power is the spiker. It is also necessary, however, to build a well-balanced team that can serve, pass, and "set up".

DEFENSIVE PLAY

The reception and handling of serves and spikes is the primary duty of the team on defense.

    a. Receiving the Serve. The forwards move to the rear of their area. The left and right backs cover the rear, the center back plays slightly forward of the other two backs.

    b. Blocking. The block is made by the center forward and either the right or left forward. The forward not executing the block must cover the position left vacant.

ABRIDGED RULES

    a. The volleyball court is 30 feet wide by 60 feet long.

    b. The top of the net is 8 feet high.

    c. A volleyball team consists of six players.

    d. A match consists of the best two out of three games.

    e. The first team scoring 15 points wins the game, provided that they have two points more than their opponents.

    f. A deuce game is a game in which both teams score 14 points. The game is continued until one team obtains a 2-point advantage over the other.

    g. Only the serving team can score. If the serving team commits a fault, it loses the serve to the opposing team.

    h. The team receiving the ball for service rotates one position in a clockwise direction.

    i. The ball is put into play by serving from behind the back line.

    j. A served ball touching the net results in the loss of the serve. At any other time during play, a ball touching the net is still in play.

    k. The ball is out of play when it touches the ground or goes outside one of the boundary lines..

    l. All line balls are good.

    m. The players must hit or bat the ball; they may not throw, lift, or scoop it.

    n. A player may not touch the ball with any part of the body below the knees.

    o. A player may not play (touch) the ball twice in succession. In receiving a hard-driven spike, a defensive player may make several contacts with the ball even if they are not simultaneous. All such contacts, however, must constitute one continuous play, and all must be above the knees.

    p. The ball may be touched no more than three times on one side of the net before being returned across the net to the opposing team.

    q. A player must not touch or reach across the net.

    r. A player may not cross the line under the net; he may touch it, however.

    s. For complete official volleyball rules, see the United States Volleyball Association: Volleyball Official Guide.

———